Challenge and Change
History of the Jews in America
The Twentieth Century and Beyond

Written by: Shelley Kapnek Rosenberg, Ed.D.

Historian and Researcher: Alice L. George, Ph.D.

Historians: Reena Sigman Friedman, Ph.D. and Michael Alexander, Ph.D.

Historical Consultant: Jonathan D. Sarna, Ph.D.

Educational Consultants, Auerbach Central Agency for Jewish Education:
Nancy M. Messinger, Rochelle Buller Rabeeya, and Helene Z. Tigay

Project Directors:
Nancy Isserman, Ph.D.
Murray Friedman, Ph.D.

This project has been conducted under the auspices of the
Myer and Rosaline Feinstein Center for American Jewish History, Temple University.

BEHRMAN HOUSE, INC.

Designer: Julia Prymak, Pryme Design   **Project Editor:** Terry Kaye, Behrman House, Inc.

Front Cover Images:

Egypt-Israel peace treaty, March 26, 1979 of President Jimmy Carter, President Anwar Sadat, and Premier Menachim Begin, Library of Congress Prints and Photographs Division, LC-DIG-ppmsca-03424 (and p. 52)

Soviet Jewry Demonstration (and p. 3 and p. 63) and Bella Abzug (and p. 68), courtesy of the Urban Archives, Temple University Libraries, Philadelphia, PA

Ethiopian wedding in Israel, courtesy of American Jewish Historical Society, Newton Center, Massachusetts and New York, New York

Back Cover Images:

IDF officer's course cadets participating in the "March of the Living" at the Auschwitz-Birkenau Nazi concentration camp in Poland, during Holocaust Memorial Day, courtesy of Moshe Milner/Israel Government Printing Office

Mrs. Avital Sharansky and World War I soldier, courtesy of American Jewish Historical Society, Newton Center, Massachusetts and New York, New York

Credits:

Share: Jewish Relief Campaign lithographed by Sackett and Wilhelms Corp., Brooklyn, NY, circa 1917, Library of Congress Prints and Photographs Division, cph 3g09664 (p. 3 and p. 4)

Map of World War I, courtesy of the Department of History, U.S. Military Academy (p. 6)

Al Jolson, *The Jazz Singer* window card advertisement, courtesy of the Museum of the City of New York (p. 12)

Swing, Mark Ellison, pencil on paper illustration for *Hank Greenberg: Hall-of-Fame Slugger*, © 1991, The Jewish Publication Society with permission of the publisher, The Jewish Publication Society (p. 13)

Sentenced to Death! pamphlet, courtesy of a private collection (p. 28)

Anti-Nazi demonstration in Madison Square Garden, 1937, courtesy of AP/Wide World Photos (p. 30)

Jewish refugee children arrive in New York from Hamburg, Germany, 1939, courtesy of AP/Wide World Photos (p. 31)

Interfaith in Action stamp, courtesy of the U.S. Postal Service (p. 32)

Map of World War II, courtesy of the Department of History, U.S. Military Academy (p. 33)

Boycott the Jewish Boycotters flyer, circa 1937, courtesy of the Community Relations Committee of the Jewish Federation Council of Los Angeles, Urban Archives Center, Oviatt Library, California State University, Northridge (p. 37)

Ethel and Julius Rosenberg, courtesy of the Urban Archives, Temple University Libraries, Philadelphia, PA (p. 38)

Memorial and plaque dedication ceremony, courtesy of Jacob Rader Marcus Center of the American Jewish Archives, Cincinnati Campus, Hebrew Union College, Jewish Institute of Religion (p. 39)

Bess Myerson seated on the Miss New York City float, Atlantic City, NJ, 1945, AP/Wide World Photos (p. 45)

Elie Wiesel, courtesy of the Urban Archives, Temple University Libraries, Philadelphia, PA (p. 45)

Nazi war criminal Adolf Eichmann in glass box at his trial in Jerusalem, courtesy of John Milli/Israel Government Printing Office (p. 48)

Map of Events leading to the Six Day War, © Koret Communications (www.koret.com) All rights reserved. (p. 51)

Natan Sharansky, AP/Wide World Photos (p. 65)

Ruth Bader Ginsburg, courtesy of Steve Petteway, Collection of the Supreme Court of the United States (p. 69)

Joseph Lieberman, courtesy of Senator Joseph Lieberman's office (p. 69)

Richard Rogers and Oscar Hammerstein II, courtesy of the Urban Archives, Temple University Libraries, Philadelphia, PA (p. 71)

The First Jewish Catalog, reprinted from *The First Jewish Catalog* by Richard Siegel, Michael Strassfeld, ©1973, The Jewish Publication Society with permission of the publisher, The Jewish Publication Society (p. 73)

Gloria Steinem, courtesy of the Urban Archives, Temple University Libraries, Philadelphia, PA (p. 74)

Di Kats der Payats, The Cat in the Hat translated into Yiddish by Sholem Berger, New York, 2003, TM © 1957, Dr. Seuss Enterprises, L.P. All rights reserved. (p. 77)

Native American advertisement for Levy's Real Jewish Rye Bread, NY, 1967, used with permission of Arnold Products, Inc. and Levy's is a registered trademark of Arnold Products, Inc. (p. 78)

All other photographs, except cover of a pamphlet, *Jewish Activities in the United States* (p. 8) and of Rabbi Abraham Heschel marching with Dr. Martin Luther King, Jr., in 1965 (p. 55), courtesy of American Jewish Historical Society, Newton Center, Massachusetts and New York, New York.

Copyright © 2005 by Behrman House, Inc.
Springfield, New Jersey
www.behrmanhouse.com

ISBN-10: 0-87441-780-5
ISBN-13: 978-0-87441-780-7
Manufactured in the United States of America

This textbook has been funded by Righteous Persons Foundation, The Farber Foundation, and private donors.

For additional resources, go to the *Challenge and Change* website at www.challengeandchange.temple.edu.

Contents

Reflect On It

What was the effect of World War I on the American Jewish community?

P eople called it the Great War, which it was in that it encompassed so much of the world. They called it The War to End All Wars, which it was not, as in many ways it set the stage for the horror that was to follow, World War II. World War I affected the American Jewish community on the battlefield and at home, and the years that were to follow—the years between two world wars—would have an even greater impact. What would the American Jewish community look like—as it became "more American," but also dealt with increasing prejudice and antisemitism?

A TRAGIC WAR

World War I broke out in the summer of 1914, close to Tisha B'Av, the fast day commemorating the destruction of the Temples in Jerusalem as well as many other tragedies in Jewish history. This war was a tragedy for the Jews of the time. European Jews were among those who suffered and died as the war swept through their countries. Thirty-two nations were eventually involved. Many American Jews traced their roots to countries at the heart of the struggle. They witnessed the destruction of their old hometowns and the misery of their families and friends.

Before the United States finally entered the war in June 1917, American Jews raised funds for Jews in Europe. In March of 1915, Russian persecution of the country's Jews had captured Jewish attention worldwide as Russia began expelling more than 600,000 Jews from their homes, crowding them onto freight cars, and taking them to distant parts of Russia. The Yiddish press and the *American Jewish Year Book* listed a series of Russian and other European Jewish towns that were "partially or wholly destroyed" by

World War I poster for the Jewish Relief Campaign

invading armies. At least 100,000 people died, families were separated, and those who survived the war often their lost homes, businesses, and their life savings.

In an effort to help, but with America still officially neutral, three American Jewish groups tried to organize relief efforts. The Union of Orthodox Jewish Congregations organized the Central Committee for the Relief of Jews Suffering through the War, the American Jewish Committee organized the American Jewish Relief Committee, and trade union organizers and socialists led the Jewish People's Relief Committee of America. The groups agreed to collect money, combine the funds, and dispense them through an organization that was a merger of all three—the American Jewish Joint Distribution Committee. The "Joint," as it was called, was led by an executive committee whose membership was evenly split between the three participating groups. A model of cooperation, the "Joint" set the stage for future collaboration throughout the Jewish community.

Jewish soldiers from Camp Upton train for World War I.

 In Leviticus 19:16 we read, "Do not stand by while your neighbor's blood is shed." A Jew is obligated to intervene to save another person when doing so does not put his or her own life at risk. How does this obligation fit with the task of the "Joint?" Why was the communal cooperation exhibited by the "Joint" important to the future of the American Jewish community?

To learn more about the "Joint," click on http://www.jdc.org.

Many American Jews had been hopeful that America would remain neutral in the European war. Quite a few of them did not want to go to war against Germany. Some German Jews still had positive feelings for their former homeland; Jacob Schiff, a major philanthropist, had stated in 1914 that he was "pro-German," though not "anti-English." Although Russia was an ally of the U.S., other Jews felt that the war was a well-deserved punishment of Russia for its treatment of the Jews. Morris Rosenfeld, a Yiddish poet wrote, "The bleeding of Russia rejoices my heart, may the Devil do to her/What she did unto me." Still others were opposed to entering the war because they believed passionately in **pacifism**.

 Pacifism is opposition to war or violence as a method of settling disputes.

By the time the United States declared war on Germany on April 6, 1917, most

American Jews were speaking out in favor of the war. Rabbi Stephen S. Wise, a leading Reform rabbi who had taken a strong pacifist position at the outbreak of hostilities, now supported President Woodrow Wilson's declaration of war. Rabbi Mordecai M. Kaplan, founder of the Reconstructionist Movement, spoke to a group at the Young Men's

What is a "Just" War?

Although the prophet Isaiah wrote, "Nation shall not lift up sword against nation, neither shall they learn war anymore" (Isaiah 2:4), Judaism is not opposed to all war. The Talmud teaches, "If someone comes to kill you, kill him first" (*Sanhedrin* 72a). Psalm 144:1 states, "Blessed is God, my rock, who trains my hands for battle, my fingers for warfare." (This verse appeared on the front page of the *London Jewish Chronicle* when war broke out.) Find out what Judaism considers a "just" war. Compare modern war situations to this Jewish standard. Are they "just" wars? Discuss this with your classmates.

Rabbi Stephen S. Wise

S S I A

C A S P I A N S E A

A

EUROPE, 1914

N

SCALE OF KILOMETERS
0   100   200   300   400   500

SCALE OF MILES
0   100   200   300   400   500

Cartographic Lab of Excellence
Department of History, United States Military Academy

Hebrew Association in June, saying, "This is a righteous war. . . . The ideal for which we are fighting is to suppress the great bully and outlaw among the nations—the German government. . . . As Jews . . . we owe it to America to stand by her in her hour of trial." A few prominent Jews, such as Rabbi Judah Magnes, remained pacifists and spoke out against America's entry into the war. Magnes's activities reduced the effectiveness of his leadership in a Jewish community concerned about charges of disloyalty. [from Jonathan Sarna, *American Judaism: A History* (New Haven: Yale University Press, 2004)]

Because of the rise of antisemitism and those who questioned their loyalty, Jews kept careful records of their contributions to the war effort. Between 200,000 and 250,000 troops served. The *American Jewish Year Book* listed 1,500 Jewish commissioned officers by name, and the Jewish press wrote about the 3,500 who died in combat.

One of the major challenges facing the American Jewish community, and the U.S. armed forces, was meeting the diverse spiritual needs of Jewish soldiers. Since there was no single Jewish religious organization equivalent to the Protestant and Catholic ones, the community had to create one. The Jewish Welfare Board (JWB) demonstrated, as the "Joint" had, how Jews of different religious beliefs could work together. One of its tasks was to create a unified military prayer book, called the *Abridged Prayer Book for Jews in the Army and Navy of the United States* (1917).

The book was not completely satisfactory to anyone. The Orthodox thought it was inappropriately short, and the Reform complained that it did not reflect their beliefs. The book was distributed widely, but after several protests, Orthodox and Reform prayer books were made available to those soldiers who wanted them. Nonetheless, the work of the JWB was important because it taught Jews of different backgrounds about one another.

 Think About It How familiar are you with the prayer books and beliefs of the other movements of Judaism, aside from the one to which you belong? Do you believe this is important? Why or why not?

The "War to End All Wars" ended on November 11, 1918, with an **armistice** between the new German republic and the Allies. The Treaty of Versailles was signed at a peace conference in Paris in 1919.

 Learn It An **armistice** is the temporary suspension of hostilities by agreement of the warring parties.

A number of well-known American Zionists, sent by the American Jewish Congress, explained why they believed a Jewish homeland in Palestine was necessary as a haven for Jews persecuted in other countries. They also collaborated with delegates from other European Jewish groups in acquiring political rights for Jews and other minority groups in the new states that had been created in Central and Eastern Europe after the war.

THE **PARADOX** OF THE POST-WAR YEARS

The end of the war brought a period of contradictions. On one hand, Jews had participated in the war and had become, and felt, much more "American." They had fought and died next to their fellow Americans, and had come in contact with non-Jews in ways and in numbers far greater than ever before. After the war, Jews and gentiles alike benefited from a period of prosperity and became part of the middle class. More Jews lived in new and better neighborhoods, found opportunities through higher education, and held **"white-collar"** positions. The children of immigrants, born in America, were beginning to outnumber their immigrant parents, and were becoming part of middle-class mainstream America.

On the other hand, both Jews and members of other minority groups faced rising prejudice and intolerance. Prior to the war, antisemitic feelings had begun to re-emerge in America. One of the most notorious instances of anti-Jewish violence was connected with the Leo Frank case in Atlanta, Georgia, in 1913. Frank, a B'nai B'rith leader and the superintendent of a pencil factory, was convicted of murdering a thirteen-year-old employee, Mary Phagan, and leaving her body in the factory's basement. Although the case against him was weak, crowds stood outside the courthouse screaming, "Hang the Jew."

The case led to the founding that year of the Anti-**Defamation** League of B'nai B'rith (ADL), an agency dedicated to fighting antisemitism in the workplace, education, and daily life. Two years later, when, unsure of Frank's guilt, the governor commuted his death sentence to life in prison, an armed mob kidnapped Frank from the jail and **lynched** him. Years later, an eyewitness confirmed what Frank's defenders had long believed: the real murderer was the main prosecution witness and Frank was innocent. The strong feelings around the case also led to the rebirth of an organization known as the Ku Klux Klan in 1915. Well known for its attacks on Jews, Catholics, and African Americans, the Klan grew slowly until the end of the war, and then its membership skyrocketed.

A **paradox** is a statement that seems to be self-contradictory but, in reality, is possibly true.

"White-collar" positions are those that do not require manual labor.

Defamation is an attack on the good name or reputation of someone or something.

"Lynched" means that a person was killed by a mob without legal authority.

Go to www.adl.org to learn more about the history of the ADL and its mission today.

After the war, people were gripped with fear and hatred of everything foreign. The 1917 Russian Revolution had stirred up fears in the United States that radicals could try to take over the government. In 1919, a series of mail bombs addressed to prominent Americans, some of whom had spoken out for immigration restrictions, confirmed these feelings. Approximately 6,000 people were investigated and arrested, but most were released due to a lack of evidence. Others, many of them Jews, were alleged to be **subversives** and deported. [from Jonathan Sarna, *American Judaism: A History* (New Haven: Yale University Press, 2004)]

Subversives want to overthrow a government in an underhanded way.

A sample of antisemitic literature

"Within three years following the close of the war, there was perhaps more antisemitic literature published and distributed in the United States than in any previous period of its history," reported the president of the Central Conference of American Rabbis. Much of it, moreover, came

Jewish Activities
in the
United States

Volume II
of
The International Jew

A Second Selection of Articles from
The Dearborn Independent

Published by
The Dearborn Publishing Co.
Dearborn, Mich.

April 1921

from a national hero, automaker Henry Ford. In 1920, Ford's newspaper, *The Dearborn Independent*, began publishing a series of columns based on *The Protocols of the Elders of Zion*, a notorious antisemitic document first published in Russia in the early twentieth century that described a supposed international Jewish conspiracy to rule the world.

The newspaper hired a detective agency to discover any wrongdoing by a Jew that could then be publicized. Jews were criticized for their financial success, their lack of conformity, and their failure to accept Christian practices. The series ran for ninety-one issues. Four books entitled *The International Jew*, compiled from the columns, reprinted the charges and hundreds of thousands of copies were distributed. Those who criticized the articles, including former Presidents William Howard Taft and Woodrow Wilson, were denounced.

Even after recognizing Ford's personal commitment to the antisemitic series, people were uncertain what to do about it. Louis Marshall, president of the American Jewish Committee, sponsored a **rebuttal**, recruited people to sign a statement asking for a halt to "the vicious propaganda"

against Jews, and, finally urged President Warren G. Harding to intervene. Attorneys for the ADL urged passing laws against the **libel** of groups. Yiddish newspapers refused to print advertisements for Ford cars and Jews refused to buy them.

It was not until 1927, after a series of lawsuits, that the newspaper **repudiated** the articles and Ford published a letter of apology, claiming that he had not been informed about the actions of the newspaper and was "deeply mortified" to learn of the series.

A **rebuttal** is an argument or evidence that proves something to be false.

Libel is an attack on the good reputation of someone by written or printed words or pictures.

Repudiated means rejected as having no authority.

Why were such accusations made and why did many people believe them? Have you ever heard false attacks on Jews? How do you feel when you hear these types of statements? What do you do when you hear someone attacking Jews or other minority groups?

THE MOOD IN THE COUNTRY WORSENS

Jews faced additional setbacks. They had entered institutions of higher learning in record numbers, but, in 1922 when Jews made up almost 22 percent of Harvard's student body, the university's president, A. Lawrence Lowell, argued that Jewish admissions to Harvard and other universities should be limited. His initial proposal was not accepted, but a year later, Harvard limited the size of the freshman class and added "character and fitness and the promise of the greatest usefulness in the future" to the admissions qualifications. That enabled Lowell to reduce Jewish admissions to 15 percent. Of the eight Ivy League universities, only two—Brown and the University of Pennsylvania—remained reasonably open to Jews. Elite women's colleges, as well as medical schools, also restricted Jewish admissions.

The International Jew: The World's Foremost Problem

What did the columns say? The May 22, 1920 column on "The Jew in Character and Business," stated, ". . . if all this power of control has been gained and held by a few men of a long-despised race, then either they are super-men whom it is powerless to resist, or they are ordinary men whom the rest of the world has permitted to obtain an undue and unsafe degree of power. . . ." The July 10 column asked the question, "Does a Definite Jewish World Program Exist?" and answered, ". . . the finances of the world are in control of Jews; their decisions and their devices are themselves our economic law. . ." It went on to state, ". . . the patriotism of the Jew . . . is very widely questioned in all the countries. . . ."

from The Noontide Press

Ask your grand-parents, parents, teachers, or other adult friends where they went to college. Try to find out whether any of these schools had a policy limiting Jewish students at any time in the school's history.

Do you live in a Jewish neighborhood? Are there other ethnic neighborhoods in your community? What, in your opinion, are the benefits and challenges of this situation?

JEWS BECOME PART OF MAINSTREAM AMERICA

In the years after 1924 Jews responded to discrimination in a variety of ways. They attended public colleges and universities such as the so-called "Jewish Harvard"—the City College of New York (which was also tuition free)—in record numbers. They organized fraternities, hotels, and clubs of their own. Jewish businesses and organizations spread news of job openings, and Jews hired and **patronized** other Jews.

Patronize means to support, often by purchasing goods from someone.

Jews faced additional restrictions from clubs, hotels, resorts, and fraternities, as well as some of the most desirable neighborhoods in many cities. Clubs in at least fifteen cities barred Jews, and most elegant hotels and resorts also discriminated against Jews. One hotel advertised itself as, "exclusively for gentiles," while another stated, "No Hebrews or tubercular guests received." Some apartments on Coney Island, New York, boasted that they were "sensibly priced, sensibly built, [and] sensibly restricted." [from Jonathan Sarna, *American Judaism: A History* (New Haven: Yale University Press, 2004)]

By 1924, the mood of the country set the scene for the National Origins Immigration (Johnson-Reed) Act. Strengthening a 1921 act that had established the principle of a country-by-country **quota** on immigrants, the Johnson-Reed Act severely limited immigration from southern and Eastern Europe, including Jewish immigration. Between 1925 and 1934, only about 8,270 Jews were admitted to the United States each year.

Another result of the exclusion Jews faced during the interwar years was the creation of neighborhoods where Jews lived next to, but apart from, non-Jews. Thus, while Jews appeared to have succeeded in America, many actually lived and worked in a separate sub-culture that was almost completely Jewish.

Quotas are parts of something that are set aside; in this case, a number of spaces set aside for Jews or members of other minority groups.

... *This is the Fourth of July, the glorious Independence Day, and it is fitting that an American citizen, one of your nephews, not by birth but one by choice, by adoption, should address you. ...*

"selected you, dear Uncle Sam, because we were tired ... of Old World jealousies and hatreds, of the old world spirit of destruction. ... we felt that here under your guidance, there might be developed a new civilization based on the broadest humanity. Here there would be an end to the religious prejudices and racial animosities which have made of the Old World a slaughterhouse. We gave more than lip-worship to you. We gave you ourselves and our children so that this country might live as an exemplar to the rest of mankind.

Is our faith to prove an illusion? Are our hopes to be dashed to the ground, shattered beyond repair? ...

Your loyal nephew,
L.L. Bril

Several businesses became distinctly Jewish. Jews who had been employed in the garment industry now purchased factories of their own. Many Jewish business owners dealt in scrap metal and other waste products, industries suited to a people who were excluded from other sectors of the economy. Real estate became an increasingly important "Jewish" business, with property owners acquiring the tenement buildings where they had once lived. Jews also owned three of the country's largest cosmetics firms—Revlon, Max Factor, and Helena Rubinstein.

Jews made many contributions to American life and culture, especially in literature, the arts, and the entertainment industry. In these professions, talent mattered more than ancestry, and Jews thrived. Not only were the entertainers themselves Jewish, they often used their Jewishness in their acts. Fanny Brice, a popular comedienne and singer, explained why she sang and spoke with a "Jewish accent": "In anything Jewish I ever did, I wasn't standing apart, making fun of the race. I was the race, and what happened to me on the stage is what could happen to them. . . . They identified with me and then it was all right to get a laugh, because they were laughing at me as much as at themselves." Some of Brice's best-loved songs were written for her by Irving Berlin, one of the most successful Jewish composers of all time. He wrote a song for her and told her to sing it with a Yiddish accent. Brice was hesitant at first because she did not speak Yiddish, but she quickly became identified with the use of this accent.

 Think About It What is your reaction to comedians telling jokes about their own race or religion? About someone else's race or religion?

Irving Berlin may have inherited his ear for music from his father, a cantor. In one of his early jobs he wrote Yiddish-English parodies for a music publisher. Eventually—and ironically—he wrote the nation's most popular Christian holiday songs, "White Christmas" and "Easter Parade." An immigrant who left Russia as a boy, he also penned one of the country's favorite patriotic songs, "God Bless America."

George Gershwin, one of the greatest geniuses of the music world, along with his brother Ira, who wrote the lyrics to his songs, was influenced by his Jewish heritage—both in his music and in its content. They turned the novel *Porgy,* about poor African Americans, into an opera because George, a son of Russian-Jewish immigrants, strongly identified with those who suffered discrimination. George also made frequent use of "blue notes," derived both from cantorial chant and African-American blues, which add a tinge of melancholy to otherwise upbeat music.

The first full-length "talking picture," *The Jazz Singer* (1927), was the fictionalized account of the life of entertainer Al Jolson [Asa Yoelson]. Based on a short story called "The Day of Atonement," the story was, at first, considered too ethnic for film and was almost not made. First turned into a Broadway show, and then a movie (remade in 1953 and 1980), *The Jazz Singer* tells the story of living in two worlds, Jewish and American, and the difficult choices that entails. In real life, Jolson was the son of a rabbi, sang jazz and ragtime, and performed minstrelsy (impersonated African Americans). When the film came out, newspapers, including African American ones, generally gave it positive reviews.

Reaction to the Immigration Act of 1924

American Jews saw the act as a racially discriminatory law. On July 4, one of New York's Yiddish newspapers printed this letter to the editor about the law. "Is Our Faith to Prove an Illusion?" was printed in an Orthodox paper, the *Yiddishes Tageblatt* [*The Jewish Daily News*].

 Do It Imagine that you are the son or daughter of a Jewish immigrant to the United States. Write a letter to the editor reacting to the Immigration Act of 1924.

Think About It What is your reaction to this Jewish immigrant's feelings?

from Jacob Rader Marcus, ed., *The Jew in the American World: A Source Book* **(Detroit: Wayne State University Press, 1996)**

Do It

See the original movie version of *The Jazz Singer*. What is your opinion of the dilemma it presents?

Jews, often known as the "People of the Book," were also becoming successful in the field of writing. Edna Ferber won the Pulitzer Prize for *So Big*, which became a best-seller, and her novel, *Show Boat,* was made into a musical show. Gertrude Stein attracted a group of writers to her Paris apartment. Known for experimenting with the sound and rhythm of words, her most famous line was "A rose is a rose is a rose is a rose," [*Geography and Plays* (Brooklyn: M.S.G. Haskell House, 1922)].

Jews became more involved in sports as well. They were successful in a sport that had once been dominated by the Irish—boxing. Attempting to escape their poor surroundings, Jewish fighters found boxing a quick way to earn money, even though it was not viewed favorably by many in the established Jewish community. Although *Who's Who in American Jewry* refused to list them, Jewish boxers were folk heroes to many young Jews, and by the 1930s Jews were the largest ethnic group in all weight divisions. In what may have been a gesture of defiance, many Jewish boxers wore a Star of David on their boxing trunks.

The boxing gloves of Benny Leonard, a famous Jewish boxer

As Jews continued to move up the economic ladder and out of the cities, they also began to look to "All American" sports like basketball and baseball for heroes. Jewish parents approved of basketball, and many high school and college teams in New York City boasted lineups that were mostly Jewish. Many of these young men became All-Americans and even professional stars.

Hank Greenberg is the best example. He was a high school star in New York City before becoming a major-leaguer.

Henry Benjamin "Hammerin' Hank" Greenberg was baseball's first Jewish superstar. In 1934, with his help, the Detroit Tigers found themselves in a pennant race, but there were games scheduled on Rosh Hashanah and Yom Kippur. While the country debated whether he should play, Greenberg came up with a compromise. He played on Rosh Hashanah, hitting two home runs

Do It

Find out about Jews who were successful in the arts, entertainment, sports, business, or politics during the interwar years. How did their Judaism influence their lives?

Molly Picon on the Maxwell House Radio Show in 1938

that helped the Tigers win the game two-to-one, and spent Yom Kippur in synagogue, while the Tigers lost. Detroit won the pennant, but lost the World Series to the St. Louis Cardinals. The Tigers won the series a year later, and Greenberg was the first Jew in either major league to be voted Most Valuable Player.

The passage of the Eighteenth Amendment on January 16, 1920, forbidding "the manufacture, sale, or transportation of intoxicating liquors," ushered in Prohibition and set the stage for the rise of Jewish gangsters who would provide what many people wanted—alcohol. The typical Jewish gangster was also involved in gambling, **extortion**, peddling narcotics, and even murder. They chose a life of crime because it was the fastest—and most daring—way to acquire money and fame, in quantities usually far beyond the dreams of middle-class Jews. The violence that was part of the lifestyle was acknowledged and accepted by these criminals.

Learn It

Extortion is forcing money or information from a person by intimidation.

Members of the Jewish community had strangely mixed feelings about its gangsters. Communal leaders feared the publicity these men attracted would kindle antisemitic anger against the entire community. And of course, people knew the gangsters' actions were wrong. Abe "Kid Twist" Reles was said to have "committed just about every act of violence against which there is a law." Yet some Jews respected men like Louis Lepke Buchalter, called by J. Edgar Hoover "the most dangerous criminal in the United States," because they had "made it" in America, competing with non-Jews and beating them at their own game. Moreover, many Jews felt they owed men like Samuel "Nails" Morton a debt of gratitude for protecting their neighborhoods from Jew-baiters. Jewish parents, however, feared their children would find the gangster lifestyle appealing and grow up to imitate the gangsters.

From culture to sports to business Jews played an important role in many areas of American life while American society greatly influenced American Jews.

Do It

Does being good to one's mother and helping other Jews make up for the mobsters' murderous crimes? In what way? Stage a debate.

Click On It

Click on The Jewish Virtual Library (www.us-israel.org), www.jewishpeople.net, or Gates to Jewish Heritage (www.jewishgates.com) to learn about Jewish gangsters.

"Hammerin' Hank": A Poem

Edgar Guest wrote a poem about Greenberg's dilemma and deliberations:

Come Yom Kippur—holy fast day wide-world over to the Jew—

And Hank Greenberg to his teaching and the old tradition true

Spent the day among his people and he didn't come to play

Said Murphy to Mulrooney, "We shall lose the game today!

We shall miss him in the infield and shall miss him at the bat,

But he's true to his religion—and I honor him for that!"

Do It

Do you agree with Greenberg's compromise? What would you have done? Do you know of any other Jews who had to make similar compromises between their careers and their Judaism? Discuss these questions with your classmates.

CHAPTER 2

DEVELOPMENTS IN THE MOVEMENTS

How did each of the Jewish religious movements develop and change in response to the environment of America?
How did the role of women in Judaism change?

The years between the World Wars were truly a time of challenge and change for the Jews of America. Most of the children of immigrants wanted to be as Americanized as possible. Many felt Jewish but were not especially interested in religious observance. They lived in Jewish neighborhoods, joined Jewish organizations, and socialized with other Jews, but few attended synagogue on a regular basis. They built a Jewish culture reflected in literature, theater, and even a popular radio program, but only a small number of Jewish children attended Jewish schools. It was a time of great concern for leaders of all segments of the Jewish community as they worked to bring Jews back to Judaism.

ORTHODOXY AND MODERNITY

Of all of the movements within Judaism, Orthodoxy faced the greatest challenge during this time. Immigration was restricted, so fewer traditionally observant Jews were reaching America's shores. Those who had arrived earlier found the free and nonjudgmental social environment of the so-called "Roaring Twenties" (the 1920s) very appealing and attractive. "Clothing was selected for style and there was less concern for its modesty. There were new foods to taste, and acceptable ways for men to pass the time in the evening and on Shabbes other than at Torah study. . . . Orthodox Jews . . . attended the theater, and courting couples could go to the movies without stirring community gossip and disapproval." [from Jonathan Sarna, *American Judaism: A History* (New Haven: Yale University Press, 2004)]. That had not been true in Orthodox communities in the past—even in America. The first yeshiva in America, the Etz Chaim Yeshiva, was founded in 1886, and was followed in 1897 by the Rabbi Isaac Elchanan Theological Seminary. One of the seminary's own students, Rabbi Bernard (Dov) Revel, led a merger of the two schools in 1915, introducing

changes he hoped would make Orthodoxy more appealing to modern, Americanized Jews. Renamed the Rabbinical College of America, the school curriculum included both Jewish and secular studies.

A few years later, Revel developed plans for a "Yeshiva College" as an extension to the existing elementary and high schools, teachers' college, and **theological** seminary. His goal was to enable students to "combine the best of modern culture with the learning and the spirit of the Torah and ideals of traditional Judaism." Later known as Yeshiva University, the school trained both American Orthodox rabbis and Orthodox lay persons—members of a group that would become known as "Modern Orthodox." In 1948, it began educating Orthodox Jewish women as well.

 Theological means related to the study of God and God's relation to the universe.

 Learn about Yeshiva University at www.yu.edu.

During the interwar years, Americanized Orthodox Jews who wanted to both maintain Judaism and adapt it to their new homeland were trying to change the atmosphere of their synagogues. As early as 1896, a group of young, American-born men in New York had recognized that their contemporaries would prefer a mostly traditional service, but without some of the **raucous** behavior typical of the old-fashioned, European-style services. Several synagogues sprang up in New York in the early 1900s to serve them.

Still, traditional synagogues were not reaching all young American Jews. Several organizations were now founded to connect with them. The Harlem Young Men's Hebrew Orthodox League, for example, established synagogues throughout the community that emphasized **decorum** and congregational singing conducted by the young people themselves, and sponsored many social, cultural, and recreational activities as well.

Orthodox leaders also became aware of the needs of the community's women. In the past, Orthodox women lived their religious lives mainly through their attention to home life and rituals. Now, however, the community was encouraging people to attend synagogue. And for many women, going to synagogue became an important part of their ritual lives. It was, said one woman, "a big deal."

It was also easier for women to enjoy and participate in the services. In the old-fashioned Orthodox synagogue, women sat in a small alcove, often separated from the main sanctuary by a heavy curtain. Women were now provided with a spacious upstairs balcony with a clear view of the *bimah*, or a space on the main floor separated from the men by a partition known as a *mechitzah*. The services themselves were now often conducted in English and Hebrew instead of Yiddish and Hebrew, and a common prayer book with English translations made participation easy.

Raucous means "wild."

Decorum means "good manners," in this case, a more formal and dignified service.

Mechitzah is the separation that divides the men's and women's sections of a traditional synagogue. It was originally derived from the women's "court" in the Temple in Jerusalem.

On the Lower East Side, founders of the "Young Israel" movement attempted to "bring about a revival of Judaism among the thousands of young Jews and Jewesses . . . whose Judaism is at present **dormant**." A group of fifteen young men and women first initiated Friday night lectures, in English, on a variety of topics of Jewish interest. Three years later, in 1915, they established a model synagogue on East Broadway that incorporated congregational singing and the use of English except for prayer. Decorum was stressed and the congregation *davened* a traditional liturgy. In order to attract even the poorest members of the community, as well as more Americanized young Jews, the congregation's leaders discouraged the traditional practice of paying for synagogue honors, such as an aliyah to the Torah. They described the new synagogue as a place where tradition could be observed in a way that appealed to young men and women.

Dormant means "inactive."

Daven is Yiddish for "pray."

You can read more about Young Israel on their website at www.youngisrael.org.

Visit a synagogue connected with each of the other movements of which you are not a member. If possible, attend a service. Speak to the rabbi and/or educational director. How is it similar to and different from the synagogue to which you belong?

CHANGES IN THE CONSERVATIVE MOVEMENT

The Jewish Theological Seminary, which became the primary training ground for rabbis who led the Conservative Movement, was, like the Etz Chaim Yeshiva, founded in 1886. A small group of rabbis was called together by Rabbi Sabato Morais, of Philadelphia's Sephardic Mikveh Israel Congregation, who became the new seminary's first president. He sought to uphold traditional Judaism and was a staunch opponent of Reform Judaism. Aware that in Central Europe, Rabbi Zechariah Frankel had developed a compromise between Orthodoxy and Reform that had been adopted by the majority of Jews in the German and Austro-Hungarian Empire, these rabbis reasoned that this model might be appropriate for America.

At the start, the seminary's founders did not set out to establish a separate **denomination** of Judaism; in fact, as one rabbi said, "Modern Orthodox congregations are frequently indistinguishable in practice and spirit from avowedly Conservative synagogues and many of their rabbis frequently **expound** a similar philosophy of Judaism." For many years some synagogues even

identified as both Conservative and Orthodox. [from Jonathan Sarna, *American Judaism: A History* (New Haven: Yale University Press, 2004)]

Rabbi Solomon Schechter, a well-known Jewish scholar, had arrived to lead JTS in 1902. Schechter was a traditionalist but believed that there could be changes in modern Judaism, as long as they were introduced for good reasons. He explained his position by saying, "The Torah gave spiritual accommodations for thousands of years to all sorts and conditions of man . . . and it should . . . prove broad enough to harbor different minds of the present century."

A **denomination** is a group of congregations which agree upon religious principles.

Expound is to "explain" or "talk about."

Should changes be introduced into modern Judaism? If so, how? What types of changes? Are there things that cannot be changed if Judaism is to remain Judaism?

Rabbi Solomon Schechter

At first, even Reform and Orthodox leaders welcomed Schechter's arrival. But, while he maintained good relations with Reform leaders, Orthodox leaders soon strongly opposed some of his actions. Agudath HaRabonim accused him of **heresy** in 1904 because the Seminary's faculty members were allowed to analyze the Torah and Talmud in a critical, academic way.

However, Schechter's flexibility appealed to many of the children of immigrants because he stressed the importance of *klal Yisra'el*, the interconnection among all Jews, while avoiding some problematic **ideological** issues. Schechter and the Conservative movement embraced Zionism as the fulfillment of their belief in

Jewish peoplehood. He and his supporters did not see Jewish law as a direct revelation from God and favored the use of modern scholarship, although they rejected some Reform interpretations. Conservative Judaism accepted the dietary laws and the requirement to observe on Shabbat, although some members of Conservative congregations did not follow these laws. The movement favored the use of Hebrew in services, approved of traditional rituals, and preferred men's wearing *kippot*. Some synagogues had family seating, instead of dividing men and women, and some included choirs, organs, and English translations of prayers.

In 1913, Schechter united sixteen Conservative congregations to form the United Synagogue of America, a congregational organization for the movement. The organization reaffirmed the authority of the Talmud as a guide to Jewish practice, emphasized the traditional observance of Shabbat and kashrut, maintained Hebrew as the primary language of prayer, expressed hope for Israel's rebirth as a nation, and supported the establishment of Jewish religious schools. These were all goals with which

Do It

Schechter stressed the importance of the Jewish community, and in *Pirkei Avot* (2:4) we read, "Do not separate yourself from the community." Reflect on these words and write your own *d'var Torah* on what this means to you. Think about the issue of conforming or not conforming to the expectations of a community.

Orthodox Jews could agree. So close were the two movements that, in 1926, there was even a serious, but unsuccessful, effort to merge the Jewish Theological Seminary and Yeshiva College.

Under Schechter's leadership, JTS hired a renowned faculty. In 1909, it initiated a Teachers Institute for training Jewish educators. When Schechter died in 1915, Cyrus Adler became president and served until 1940. Adler, who was also president of United Synagogue, was particularly effective in bridging the gap between traditional Jewish scholarship and modern American Judaism.

The Conservative movement grew considerably during the years between the two World Wars, moving further away from Orthodoxy as both movements tried in their own ways to meet the challenges life in America presented to Judaism. The Orthodox Union was increasingly reluctant to support innovations that JTS-trained rabbis wanted to introduce in order to attract young people. The underlying issues, however, that pulled the movements apart were questions of rabbinic authority, the role of the Talmud, women's rights, and the extent to which Jewish law could be bent to meet the challenges of modern life.

An example of one of the innovations introduced in Conservative congregations was mixed seating. Reform congregations had already eliminated separate seating for men and women in order to demonstrate their commitment to women's equality and attract younger Jews to the synagogue. Now, JTS-trained rabbis considered doing the same. Although Adler and some seminary professors disapproved, mixed seating, sometimes with accommodations for people who preferred to sit apart, became popular.

RECONSTRUCTING JUDAISM

While Orthodox Judaism made few changes in response to life in America, and Conservative Judaism made more changes, one man, Rabbi Mordecai M. Kaplan proposed, "the introduction of radical and sweeping changes" in Judaism. Kaplan had received his rabbinical ordination from the Jewish Theological Seminary and went on to teach there for fifty-four years. Kaplan, who began his career as an Orthodox rabbi and was one of the founders of the Young Israel movement, soon began to feel that he "could no longer preach and teach according

Think About It

What type of seating does your synagogue have? Have you ever attended services at a synagogue with different seating?

to Orthodox doctrine." In a 1920 article entitled "A Program for the Reconstruction of Judaism," Kaplan called for a movement to "**revitalize** the entire system of ceremonial observances by adjusting them to the spiritual needs of our day."

In 1922, Kaplan founded the Society for the Advancement of Judaism (SAJ). He felt that "society" was a more appropriate term than "synagogue" because he hoped to start "a group of communities . . . with large numbers of . . . followers who were not limited to the local community." Kaplan's *Judaism*, which he described in his 1934 book *Judaism As a Civilization: Toward a Reconstruction of American-Jewish Life*, centered on the Jewish people, rather than God or Jewish law. He focused on "Jewish civilization," which he defined as "embracing every Jew and everything Jewish including land (Israel), history, language, literature, religious folkways, **mores**, law, and art." Jews, he said, needed to "rediscover, reinterpret, and reconstruct" their civilization. Kaplan was convinced that the "reconstructed" synagogue would play a crucial role in saving Judaism in America. Merging the social, cultural, and recreational activities of the YMHA with the religious activities of the synagogue, he believed,

would attract young Jews who were not interested in their parents' Judaism.

Learn It

Revitalize means to refresh or renew.

Mores means traditions, or customs.

Kaplan's ideas were controversial. Particularly so were his redefining God in non-supernatural terms as "the power that makes for salvation," his denial of the concept of Jews as a nation "chosen" by God, and his willingness to discard or change Jewish practices that, he felt, had "outlived their usefulness." These ideas, however, were exactly what appealed to many people. Ultimately, they led to the creation of a new movement known as Reconstructionism, the only Jewish movement that had no European roots and developed completely within the United States. While most American Jews did not become Reconstructionists, Kaplan's ideas influenced the other movements, as well as other areas of Jewish life. Several of his ideas—for example, that "tradition should have a vote, but not a veto,"—stimulated debate that helped to further distinguish the Orthodox from the Conservative movement, especially when the Agudath HaRabonim excommunicated him in 1945 after the publication of his *Sabbath Prayer Book*. [from Jonathan Sarna, *American Judaism: A History* (New Haven: Yale University Press, 2004)]

Two of Kaplan's ideas became common across all of American Jewish life. First, was the notion that Judaism was a "religious civilization." Kaplan insisted that Jewish art, craft, drama, music, food, and dance were as important to Jewish life as were religious laws, ceremonies, and rituals. A related idea was that of the "synagogue-center," a multipurpose facility open seven days a week, that would serve as a hub of Jewish community life. Although Kaplan did not invent this notion, he explained it, saying that the synagogue "must become the Jew's second home." The Jewish Center—part synagogue,

Do It

Do you agree that "tradition should have a vote, but not a veto?" Prepare to debate this idea.

part social hall, part athletic club—founded in 1918 on Manhattan's West Side with Kaplan as its leader, set the pattern for what would become known as the synagogue-center movement, with congregations that included a full range of religious, social, cultural, educational, and recreational services for people of all ages.

Go to www.rrc.edu, the website of the Reconstructionist Rabbinical College, for more information about Reconstructionist philosophy.

Find out whether any synagogues in your community were part of the synagogue-center movement. What facilities and activities did they offer? How is your synagogue similar to or different from the synagogue-center model? What is your opinion of this type of synagogue? Design your own synagogue-center. What would it include?

REFORM JUDAISM REFORMS

In 1903, Kaufmann Kohler had become president of Hebrew Union College and reinforced many practices that had become common in many Reform synagogues, such as the banning of *kippot* and *tallitot* within the seminary. He opposed discussion of Zionism and forbade the use of some prayers. He also helped shape the college into a stronger seminary, requiring that faculty members work full time and hold doctorates. His successor, Julian Morgenstern, continued the push for academic excellence.

As time went on, however, it became increasingly clear to Reform rabbis serving congregations around the country that the movement needed to change. Many advocated a return to more traditional practices and a greater emphasis on Jewish peoplehood. Partly in response to Kaplan's ideas,

and also as a result of the dissatisfaction being expressed by their members, some congregations introduced elements of the synagogue-center concept, while others, in an effort to attract more of the Eastern European immigrants, reintroduced such discarded rituals as the bar mitzvah.

Reform Jews had begun showing an interest in Zionism; by the 1920s about half of Reform rabbis openly supported Zionism. Felix Levy, a staunch Zionist, became president of the Central Conference of American Rabbis (CCAR) in 1935. Previously, Reform Judaism had stressed that Judaism was a religion and not a nation. The 1937 Columbus Platform, which replaced the Pittsburgh Platform as the defining statement of the Reform movement, spoke repeatedly of the "Jewish people," and stressed the idea that Judaism included both **ethnicity** and faith. The platform's statement on Israel described Judaism as "the soul of which Israel is the body," and declared, "We affirm the obligation of all Jewry to aid in its upbuilding as a Jewish homeland by endeavoring to make it not only a haven of refuge for the oppressed but also a center of Jewish culture and spiritual life. . . ."

Rabbi Stephen S. Wise, a dedicated Zionist, was one of the Reform movement's primary leaders during the interwar years. Desiring complete **freedom of the pulpit**, he founded the Free Synagogue, and addressed thousands every Sunday morning at New York's Carnegie Hall. He helped to organize the American Jewish Congress as a pro-Zionist alternative to the non-Zionist American Jewish Committee, and founded a new rabbinical seminary, the Jewish Institute of Religion, in 1922. The school's students believed in the three major ideas that Wise supported: Zionism, social justice, and the notion of serving the Jewish people as a whole. In fact, the CCAR took increasingly strong social action stands during the interwar years. It backed such causes as the minimum wage, the eight-hour workday, and workers' compensation for those injured in work-related accidents, and it condemned corruption and monopolies in business.

Ethnicity refers to "a group of people of the same race or nationality who share distinctive cultural characteristics."

Freedom of the pulpit means that a congregation's spiritual leader may express his or her opinions freely without restraint from the congregation's lay leadership.

The Columbus Platform: The Guiding Principles of Reform Judaism

The Columbus Platform stated: "Prayer is the voice of religion . . . To deepen the spiritual life of our people, we must cultivate the traditional habit of communion with God through prayer in both home and synagogue." It also called for "the preservation of the Sabbath, festivals and Holy Days, the retention and development of such customs, symbols and ceremonies as possess inspirational value, the cultivation of distinctive forms of religious art and music[,] and the use of Hebrew, together with the vernacular, in our worship and instruction."

Click On It

To read the entire Columbus Platform, click on www.challengeand-change.temple.edu. Go to primary documents, click on the links, then click on The Guiding Principles of Reform Judaism under the Central Conference of American Rabbis Platforms.

Do It

List principles of the section of the Columbus Platform found above. Find out about the movement today. What additional changes have taken place? What remains the same? If you do not belong to the Reform movement, how is it similar to or different from the movement to which you belong?

Think About It

Do you think rabbis should or should not take stands on secular matters of social justice? Does it violate the idea of separation of church and state or is it an example of living by *middot* [Jewish virtues]?

The Reform movement significantly improved the Jewish education by providing a professional journal, new textbooks, and a new curriculum that included Jewish customs and ceremonies, Hebrew language, and Zionism. The movement also paid special attention to the needs of women. Jane Evans was appointed executive director of the National Federation of Temple Sisterhoods in 1933, and she greatly expanded the role of the sisterhood. She advocated the formal training of women for leadership and encouraged them to participate in a wide variety of synagogue activities. Evans also encouraged women to become more active and knowledgeable Jews, and to strengthen the Jewishness of their homes.

CHANGING ROLES OF WOMEN

Women's roles in all movements of Judaism were clearly changing in the years after World War I. Previously, although a few women had received formal training at Jewish schools of higher education, none had hoped or expected to become a rabbi. The ordination of women did not receive serious attention until 1921, when Martha Neumark, a student at the Hebrew Union College and the daughter of an HUC professor, asked her teachers to let her know "where she stood" on the issue of ordination as a Reform rabbi.

The faculty of the college and the CCAR concluded that there was no reason that a woman should be barred from becoming a rabbi. When, however, an expert on Jewish law stated that ordaining women was contrary to Jewish tradition, the college's board of governors decided to continue the policy of ordaining only men. Helen Levinthal Lyons completed all of the Jewish Institute of Religion's graduation requirements in 1939, but Stephen Wise would not allow her to be ordained.

A milestone for women was achieved on March 18, 1922, when Judith Kaplan, daughter of Reconstructionist leader Mordecai Kaplan, became the first bat mitzvah in the United States at the Society for the Advancement of Judaism. The twelve-year-old girl recited a blessing, read a part of the Torah *parashah* in both Hebrew and English, and then recited the final blessing. Her father hoped that the event would help achieve greater equality for women. Recalling the brief, simple ceremony, she said, "That was enough to shock a lot of people, including

Celebrating Ḥanukkah at Radcliffe in 1945

my own grandparents and aunts and uncles." But, she also reported that, "No thunder sounded, no lightning struck, and the rest of the day was all rejoicing."

 The *parashah* is a portion of the Torah read in the synagogue each week.

Women's roles in synagogue life also expanded through their sisterhoods. Women had been banding together to form sisterhoods for many years. Now, religious leaders across the movements called on them to help prevent assimilation and revive Jewish life in America by showing that Judaism could exist in harmony with modern American values and emphasizing the special role of women in preserving and transmitting Judaism. Women helped promote social interaction among synagogue members, maintained and improved religious education, raised much-needed funds, and helped to attract unaffiliated

Ask an older female relative or teacher whether she became a bat mitzvah. What does she remember about it? How was it different from a bat mitzvah ceremony today? Have you become a bat mitzvah? Write about your own bat mitzvah and/or that of the adult you interviewed.

Do It

women to synagogue activities. They also worked on education, publications, and fundraising for their movements, and raised money for Jews around the world.

Just as synagogue life was changing for women during the interwar years, so was Jewish home life. According to the book, *The Jewish Home Beautiful,* by this time, there was little to distinguish many Jewish homes from those of non-Jewish Americans. Where once the home of the Jewish immigrant was filled with Jewish objects, the middle-class American Jewish home had "few objects of Jewish character." "The . . . picture of Theodor Herzl or Moses . . . has given way to copies of Van Goghs and Renoirs. . . . Where once a gilt-framed picture of a Jewish grandparent had hung prominently in the living room . . . 'after a few years we found it didn't look so nice with the new furniture, and so zeda [grandfather] was relegated to the bedroom. A Van Gogh print was put in his place.'" Furthermore, "cherished copper pots formerly used for making gefilte fish now served as planters, while brass candlesticks, no longer in active service as ritual implements adorned bookshelves."

This situation greatly alarmed many religious leaders, including Mathilde Schechter, the wife of Solomon Schechter, and Mordecai Kaplan. They believed that bringing Jews back to Judaism could only be accomplished when Judaism was central to the Jewish home. "Earnest rabbis and teachers are doing their best from the pulpit . . . to turn the tide, but they and the Synagogues are helpless, unless the women of Israel create Jewish homes again," Mathilde Schechter said. Books, such as *The Jewish Home Beautiful* and *The Three Pillars,* guided women in the creation of an appropriate Jewish home. As *The Jewish Home Beautiful* put it, "With woman as priestess to tend to its altars, each home is a Temple, each hearth is a shrine." [from Jenna Weissman Joselit, "The Jewish Home Beautiful" in Jonathan D. Sarna, *The American Jewish Experience* (New York: Holmes & Meier, 1997)]

The National Council of Jewish Women celebrate sukkot.

Blessing of the Sabbath candles during a
B'nai Brith Youth Organization summer convention in 1959

Why is it important for Jews to create a Jewish home? What objects make it obvious that a home is Jewish?

CONFLICTS AND COMMONALITIES

The interwar years were a time of conflict among the different movements of Judaism and within each of them. Yet it was also a time when Jews realized that there were important similarities that could unite them. Jews embraced a typical American lifestyle, but often lived apart from their Christian neighbors in neighborhoods with a distinctive Jewish culture. They wanted their synagogues to be more than simply houses of worship, and struggled with commitments to both tradition and modern life. Many supported the creation of a Jewish state in Palestine and the belief that Jews should be strong supporters of social causes. Most of all, feelings of *klal Yisra'el*—Jewish peoplehood—brought them together.

What brings you together with other Jews? Is being part of the Jewish community important to you? Is it important to have a united community? Why?

CHAPTER 3

AMERICA, AMERICAN JEWS, AND WORLD WAR II

Reflect On It

What was the effect of the Great Depression on American Jews?
How did Jews in the United States respond to the crisis of World War II?

Just as American Jews seemed to be moving into the middle class and building a better life for themselves, disaster struck. The stock market crash, the Great Depression, and World War II had an effect on all Americans. The rise of antisemitism and the devastation of the Holocaust particularly affected Jews. These were difficult times and there were difficult decisions to make.

HARD HIT BY THE CRASH AND THE DEPRESSION

During the 1920s, the nation enjoyed an economic boom. People speculated in the stock market and believed that their life savings were safe in their banks. The stock market crash in 1929 affected mainly the wealthiest people in the Jewish community. Continuing declines in stock prices and the failure of the Bank of the United States on December 11, 1930, hit many more. Many people in all economic brackets lost their life savings during what came to be known as the Great Depression.

Thousands of small businesses that had been established by Jewish immigrants were forced to close, and larger companies either shut down or laid off workers. Labor unions, many of which had significant Jewish memberships, experienced sharp declines in membership. Because layoffs were heaviest among blue-collar workers, most Jews, who were no longer manual laborers, suffered less unemployment than others. Yet Jewish workers were hit hard. In many cases, families were forced back into sweatshop-type work, and some people began peddling door to door. Wages dropped and the length of the workweek climbed back to fifty-five and even sixty hours. Jewish applications for charity increased 42 percent in just the first nine months of 1931.

When people were unable to pay dues or tuition, synagogues and Jewish educational institutions were left with expensive buildings, deficit budgets, and faculty members who could not be paid. The income of charitable institutions dropped by more than half and most campaigns to help Jews in other countries stopped during these years. Even so, most Jews were able to survive by relying on the Jewish community. Jews took pride in helping other Jews, and few had to do without necessities. Synagogues took in the homeless, the Hebrew Immigrant Aid Society (HIAS) assisted those who needed food and shelter, special fundraising campaigns were started, and communities formed employment bureaus that especially helped Jews who wanted to observe Shabbat. For the first time, however, the number of Jewish people who needed aid was so great that government support was also necessary for some.

ANTISEMITISM DURING THE '30s

Although many second generation Jews, the children of immigrants, were college-educated and had professional jobs, pre-existing antisemitism kept some jobs closed to Jews, including positions in banks, large businesses, major law firms, and on university faculties. Private universities initiated quotas for Jewish admissions. The medical field was particularly influenced by the growing antisemitic

Do It

Following are several quotes expressing the Jewish view of giving and accepting help in times of financial need. In Deuteronomy (15:7-8) we read, "If . . . there is a needy person among you . . . you must open your hand and lend him sufficient for whatever he needs."
Likewise, Leviticus (25:35-37) counsels, "When your brother Israelite is reduced to poverty and cannot support himself in the community, you shall uphold him . . ."

In the *Shulkhan Arukh* Rabbi Joseph Karo gave advice to the poor (*Yoreh Deah* 255:2): "Whoever cannot survive without taking charity, such as an old, sick, or greatly suffering individual, but who stubbornly refuses to accept aid, is guilty of murdering himself . . . yet one who needs charity but postpones taking it and lives in deprivation so as to not trouble the community, shall live to provide for others."

Write a *d'var Torah* about the Jewish view of giving and receiving help in times of financial need.

_____
_____
_____
_____
_____
_____
_____
_____
_____
_____
_____
_____
_____
_____
_____
_____

sentiment, and those Jews who won admission to medical schools discovered when they graduated that few hospitals would offer them internships. Antisemitism was also widespread in the insurance industry, where Jews were mainly restricted to selling to other Jews. Anti-Jewish references in want ads reached a peak in 1938.

As the atmosphere of antisemitism grew during the Depression, several people became well known for their antisemitic views. Between 1930 and 1942, Father Charles E. Coughlin, a Roman Catholic priest was a national radio personality. He warned his listeners of a Communist conspiracy in the United States, attacked the "international bankers"—code words for Jews—and condemned Jewish success in radio, the press, and finance. His weekly newspaper, *Social Justice*, published excerpts from the *Protocols of the Elders of Zion*. The Christian Front, a group that he established and encouraged, held violent antisemitic rallies, leading to increased street violence against Jews.

Think About It

How should Jews respond to antisemitic actions?

Lindbergh Addresses a Rally

Lindbergh spoke to an America First rally in 1941 saying: The three most important groups who have been pressing this country toward war are the British, the Jews, and the Roosevelt Administration. . . . Instead of agitating for war, the Jewish groups in this country should be opposing it in every possible way, for they will be among the first to feel its consequences. . . . The greatest danger to this country lies in [the Jews'] large ownership and influence in our motion pictures, our press, our radio, and our government.
[from Howard M. Sachar, *A History of the Jews in America* (New York: Vintage Books, 1993)]

Think About It

Why might it have been especially problematic for American Jews that a recognized hero such as Lindbergh would make such antisemitic remarks?

Charles Lindbergh, already an American hero for the first-ever solo flight across the Atlantic Ocean, also became known for his antisemitic views. Lindbergh, who with his wife, heiress Anne Morrow, visited Berlin twice in the mid-1930s, admired the "effectiveness" of Hitler's Nazi government. An **isolationist**, Lindbergh became a spokesman for America First, a group that opposed American involvement in World War II. Angered by media coverage of his baby son's abduction and murder in 1935, he now blamed supposed Jewish control of the press, the entertainment industry, and the government for leading Americans to consider entering the war.

 An **isolationist** believes in withdrawing his or her country from any alliances or commitments to other nations.

JEWS ON THE LEFT

Many Jewish students and recent college graduates were attracted to **Communism** and the **Communist** Party. The Communists appealed directly to Jews on issues of Jewish concern, and successfully **infiltrated** the white-collar, heavily Jewish unions of teachers, social workers, office workers, government employees, and retail clerks. While few Jews actually joined the party, those who did were impressed by the opportunity to demonstrate their **idealism**. Historians now know, as a result of information obtained from recently opened Soviet files, that the Communist Party leadership in the U.S. was often heavily engaged in spying, even as rank-and-file members were often idealistic and well-meaning.

Most American rabbis, some of whom were interested in **socialism** during this time, remained firmly anti-Communist during the 1920s and 1930s. Rabbi Stephen Wise gave strong sermons against Communism and conducted a successful campaign to remove Communists from leadership roles in the American Jewish Congress.

Jewish writers during the Depression were among those who wrote America's first **proletariat** literature. Michael Gold penned short stories that he turned into an autobiographical novel called *Jews without Money*. It is the story of a family that comes to America with high hopes, only to find it a land of poverty, class oppression, and brutality. Reprinted eleven times in its first year, it has been translated into fifteen languages.

Social protest was also popular on the stage. A small troop of actors formed the Group Theater and produced some of the period's most thought-provoking social dramas. *Waiting for Lefty*, by Clifford Odets, was inspired by a taxi strike in New York. The actors spoke directly to the audience, as if they were taking part in a union meeting, and the play ended with the call to "Strike! Strike! Strike!" The play was a success and soon opened on Broadway.

Do It

Discuss with grandparents, parents, or teachers why some Jews were attracted to Communism during the interwar years and why many considered the Communist Party so dangerous.

 The **Left** indicates a liberal or radical political position.

Communism is a theory of organizing a society. Under communism as it was originally conceived, there is no private ownership, and labor is organized for the common benefit of all members of society so that each should work according to his or her ability and receive according to his or her wants. A **communist** society is one in which the government controls all economic and social activity. As practiced in the Soviet Union, it involved a sharp reduction of individual rights and freedom and the harsh persecution of those who challenged the government.

To **infiltrate** is to move into an organization secretly.

Idealism is the perception of people and things as they should be rather than as they are.

Socialism is a theory of social organization based on common ownership of property.

The **proletariat** is the industrial working class.

JEWISH AMERICANS TURN TO ROOSEVELT AND THE DEMOCRATS

When Democrat Franklin Delano Roosevelt became president of the United States on March 4, 1933, he initiated the New Deal, a series of domestic programs designed to help Americans cope with the hardships of the Depression. Al Smith, the previously unsuccessful Democratic party nominee for president, had drawn Jews to the Democrats. Now, most Jews backed Roosevelt who, as governor of New York State had adopted Smith's liberal policies with the help of his lieutenant governor, Herbert Lehman. Wealthy Jews in New York's Democratic Party, including Lehman, helped raise money for Roosevelt in the 1932 primary and the Yiddish press **endorsed** him. Eighty-two percent of Jewish votes nationwide were cast for Roosevelt, a percentage not equaled by any other ethnic group. Lehman then ran for and won the governorship of New York, becoming the first Jew to hold that office.

The New Deal was designed to rescue unemployed workers, as much as banks, businesses, and employers. One change that directly affected American Judaism was the move from a six-day workweek to a five-day workweek. Religious leaders and unions with many Jewish members had been pushing for this since World War I, agreeing that it would "save the Sabbath for the Jew," "add health and strength to the American people," and "promote the home and home life." It also became a goal for those who wanted to reduce overproduction and unemployment. President Roosevelt's New Deal championed the idea, and in 1938 the Fair Labor Standards Act made it the law in many industries. While this did not automatically result in more Jews becoming Sabbath observant, those who wanted to could do so more easily. Most important, this meant that Jews would not have to choose between their religion and the common American standard of work. [from Jonathan D. Sarna, *American Judaism: A History* (New Haven: Yale University Press, 2004)]

Endorse means to "support actively."

Until the move to a five-day workweek, a number of Reform Jews were discussing shifting Shabbat to Sunday. Why might some people have proposed this change? What is your opinion of the idea?

When President Roosevelt took office, he brought with him as many talented people of various religions and ethnicities as he could, undeterred by any bigotry lingering in the country. As governor of New York, he had come to admire a number of progressive Jews, and as president he relied on their commitment to his social programs. Between 4,000 and 5,000 Jews worked for the federal government during the 1930s, and their influence was noteworthy. Some of the many talented Jews who came to Washington became members of the president's inner circle. Roosevelt also worked closely with Justice Louis Brandeis on the social reforms that Brandeis cherished, and appointed a second Jew, Felix Frankfurter, to the Supreme Court in 1939. This Jewish involvement and visibility in the New Deal had an impact on the later Jewish response to the Holocaust. It resulted in very positive Jewish feelings toward Roosevelt and hesitance on the part of some Jews to speak out in favor of rescue schemes for European Jews.

WORLD JEWRY FACES NAZISM

Adolf Hitler's 1933 rise to power in Germany signaled danger for Jews in Germany and the surrounding countries in Europe. In 1939, as Germany stood on the brink of war, Hitler promised that the war's result would be the annihilation of the "Jewish race." When Germany invaded Poland that September, hundreds of Polish Jews were killed and thousands were beaten. Hitler's troops destroyed synagogues, looted Jewish-owned shops, and stole from Jewish homes. *The Times* of London reported that Hitler had set aside an area of German-occupied Poland and planned to send Jews there from every nation that Germany occupied during the war. The report stated that it was clear that this would become "a place for gradual extermination."

After Hitler's troops marched through Norway, Denmark, the Netherlands, Belgium, Luxembourg, and France, Great Britain was the only powerful nation still standing against Hitler. The United States did not enter the war until December 1941, after the Japanese, who were Hitler's allies, launched a surprise attack on American forces at Pearl Harbor, in Hawaii. On January 20, 1942, at the Wannsee Conference in Germany, officials announced "the final solution to the Jewish problem." Through planned extermination in death camps and forced labor camps, six million Jews, one-third of the Jewish people, had been murdered by the end of the war.

As their rights were revoked and they faced increasing persecution and violence, German Jews tried desperately to leave their homeland. The German government charged a tax on their possessions, and by mid-1938, many people had lost their businesses and virtually everything they owned. Since American law banned anyone who was likely to need government assistance from entering the country, there was reason to reject them. Nevertheless, America accepted more than 200,000 Jewish refugees between 1933 and 1945. While this was more than any other country, it was still only a small number of those who might have been saved.

America's tough immigration laws, which set quotas on the number of immigrants accepted from individual nations, were still in effect. Although Jewish pressure for liberalizing the quotas grew, Congress was reluctant to do so after a 1938 survey showed that fewer than 5 percent of Americans favored such action. Moreover, more than 25 percent of American Jews admitted that they, too, would have voted against a bill to allow more European refugees into the U.S. Perhaps they feared that a new wave of Jewish immigration would add to their own economic problems and the anti-semitism that—with more than 120 organizations devoted to promoting anti-Jewish hatred—remained strong. [from Jonathan D. Sarna, *American Judaism: A History* (New Haven: Yale University Press, 2004)]

What Did People Know and When?

The problems of the Great Depression diverted the American Jewish community's attention from what was happening elsewhere in the world. In 1932, however, the *American Jewish Year Book* stated that the German-Jewish situation was a "world-shocking catastrophe" of "momentous significance to Jews everywhere." By 1935, it warned of a "deliberate premeditated policy . . . ruthlessly to exterminate German Jewry . . ." Four years later, it informed its readers "that the Nazi Government was bent upon annihilating the last **vestiges** of the German-Jewish community." Its conclusion, in 1939, was that Germany would "not rest with the annihilation of the Jewish community within her own frontiers, but sought insofar as it was able, to visit the same fate upon Jews all over the world."

How many people read these warnings is unknown. Other American, and even some Jewish and Jewish-owned newspapers, considering the reports exaggerated, either did not report the news of the Holocaust, understated German atrocities, or buried it on the inside pages. Too many people, therefore, dismissed the reports in the *Year Book* as being "beyond belief." [from Jonathan D. Sarna, *American Judaism: A History* (New Haven: Yale University Press, 2004)]

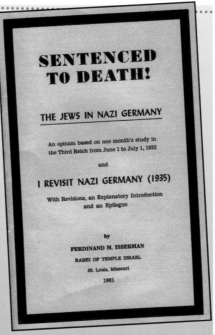

A pamphlet exposing the Nazis' treatment of Jews in Germany is ignored.

Learn It A **vestige** is a trace or visible evidence of something that is no longer in existence.

ROOSEVELT ADMINISTRATION POLICIES

President Roosevelt responded to the Jewish refugees' plight with what has become known as "the politics of gestures." He loudly voiced his sympathy, but took relatively insignificant steps to help. When, for example he called in 1938 for a conference on the refugee problem, he alerted participating nations that the United States would reject any proposed alterations to its immigration policy and that no other nation would be pressured into increasing quotas. A number of potential resettlement havens were considered, but little came of these proposals.

Another incident involved the *St. Louis*, a ship in the Hamburg-America line. The ship sailed from Hamburg, Germany, to Cuba with 930 Jews among its 1,936 passengers in May 1939. Although the refugees had paid for documents allowing them to enter Cuba, most were not allowed into the country. After sitting within sight of Miami, because the United States also refused to receive them, the ship eventually returned to Europe and most of the passengers died as the Nazis overran the countries in which they had found refuge.

The U.S. State Department also made it increasingly difficult for refugees to enter the country. Especially after June 1941, administrative procedures were tightened so that many of those who might have been admitted were denied visas. These measures were justified because of security concerns.

As evidence of Germany's policy of genocide mounted, public pressure for a more effective rescue policy grew in both Congress and Roosevelt's administration. Meanwhile, the office of Henry Morgenthau, FDR's secretary of the treasury, had been collecting data showing that the State Department was intentionally suppressing information about Hitler's "final solution," sabotaging rescue proposals, and keeping Jewish immigrants out of the United States. In a January 1944 "Report to the Secretary on the **Acquiescence** of This Government in the Murder of the Jews," the Treasury Department's legal counsel argued that unless drastic measures were taken immediately, the U.S. government would "have to share for all time responsibility" for the complete extermination of the Jews in German-controlled Europe. Roosevelt then quickly relieved the State Department of control over refugee policy and established the War Refugee Board to work with Jewish organizations to rescue refugees.

 Acquiescence means consent or agreement.

In the spring of 1944, the Treasury Department urged that the United States offer "temporary havens" within its borders for refugees. Roosevelt hesitated to do this in an election year, but after the idea was backed by a number of prominent Americans, he lent his support to such a haven in Oswego, New York. It became home to about 1,000 refugees, almost all of whom were Jews. Before entering the country, however, they were required to promise that they would return home at the end of the war. (Harry Truman, Roosevelt's successor, granted the Oswego refugees the right to remain in the United States in 1945.)

AMERICAN JEWS RESPOND TO NAZISM

During the years leading up to Pearl Harbor, some Jewish organizations tried to persuade the Roosevelt administration to help the Jews of Europe, while others hesitated to take any actions that might be an **impetus** to new American antisemitism. Key organizations collaborated in 1933, however, to form the Joint Conference Committee, designed to address the treatment of Jews in Nazi Germany. At first the committee ruled out public protest, fearing it might worsen the situation. But, when Germany's Reichstag announced the Nazis' triumphant rise to power, Rabbi Stephen Wise organized a protest rally at New York's Madison Square Garden insisting that, "the time for caution and prudence is past. We must speak up like men. How can we ask our Christian friends

New York City's Madison Square Garden is the site of a massive Nazi boycott rally on March 15, 1937.

to persuade the Amateur Athletic Union not to permit its athletes to participate, Brundage defended the group's position, saying, "Shall the American athlete be made a martyr to a cause not his own? . . . Certain Jews must now understand that they cannot use these Games as a weapon in their boycott against the Nazis. . . . Jewry suffers from . . . the self-seeking of a few in its ranks who put their personal advantage before the welfare of the race."

When it became clear that the American delegation would compete, the Committee on Fair Play sent a group of American athletes—both Jewish and non-Jewish—to Barcelona to participate in a "People's Olympics." In August, Charles Ornstein, a Jew who had been dropped from the United States Olympic Committee, presided over a "Jewish Olympiad" held on New York's Randall's Island.

to lift their voices in protest . . . if we keep silent? . . . It is not the German Jews who are being attacked. It is the Jews." [from Howard M. Sachar, *A History of the Jews in America* (New York, Vintage Books, 1993)]

One week later, Nazi leaders, blaming American-Jewish propaganda, launched a boycott against Jewish merchants. The American Jewish Committee and B'nai B'rith leaders agreed that the American protest caused the boycott. Wise rejected this notion and helped initiate a counter-boycott on German-made merchandise. While this could not weaken the German economy, it kept the issue before the American public and ensured that American Jews remained involved.

 An **impetus** is a moving or motivating force.

 Do you think it was better to protest publicly or to work quietly behind the scenes?

Rabbi Wise also asked the American representatives to the International Olympic Committee to cancel American participation in the 1936 Olympic Games scheduled for Berlin. Avery Brundage, leader of the American delegation, believed that sports transcended politics and felt embarrassed that the "Jewish issue" marred the Olympics. He barely raised the issue with Germany. When the American Jewish Congress attempted

 Should the United States have participated in the 1936 Olympics?

For the most part, those refugees who reached American shores had the help of relatives and friends. Special efforts were made to find the refugees jobs within the Jewish community, since competition with non-Jews for jobs would only increase antisemitism and pressure to bar new immigrants completely.

In 1942, Rabbi Wise received a telegram from the World Jewish Congress in Switzerland concerning the German plan to annihilate the Jews. After confirming the information with the State Department, Wise informed the press that the Nazis had killed two million Jews in an "extermination campaign." Jews organized a day of mourning and prayer, and met with Roosevelt to ask for his support.

Other efforts to arouse public sympathy for the Jews of Europe included the reporting of Nazi atrocities in Jewish newspapers, a public protest in Washington, D.C., by some 500 Orthodox rabbis, and Ben Hecht's 1943 play, *We Will Never Die*. Conceived of as a memorial to the murdered Jews, the play features groups of Jewish dead telling their stories. It ends with the chanting of the

Kaddish, the prayer for the dead. After being presented at Madison Square Garden and broadcast nationally on the radio, it went on a national tour, reaching an audience of some 100,000 people.

The Joint Distribution Committee worked closely with the War Refugee Board to save refugees. Generous contributions from individual Jews allowed the "Joint" to finance efforts that the U.S. government would not, such as helping Cardinal Angelo Roncalli (later Pope John XXIII) save 3,000 Jewish families in Hungary by providing them with false baptismal certificates, and providing $100,000 to Raoul Wallenberg, a famous non-Jewish Swedish diplomat, to save Jews in Hungary.

Jewish refugee children wave at the Statue of Liberty.

 Think About It Did American Jews do enough to save Jews during the Holocaust? What might you have done?

AMERICAN JEWISH SOLDIERS IN WORLD WAR II

Jews played a significant role in the United States armed forces during the war. In all, 550,000 Jewish citizens served in the military, many as officers, including nineteen generals and three admirals. Approximately 8,000 were killed in action and 36,000 received awards for bravery. The Jewish Welfare Board supplied Jewish chaplains and organized religious services; especially memorable was a Passover seder in 1945 held in the abandoned castle of Nazi Propaganda Minister Joseph Goebbels. Recognizing that it was serving a diverse Jewish community, the JWB also provided Jewish soldiers with prayer books, Bibles, kosher food, Jewish literature, and educational programs.

As in other wars, service in the armed forces brought up some important questions for American Jews. While most waited to be **drafted**, some chose to enlist, in some cases battling antisemitism in order to do so. A Columbia Law School graduate found that, "All my non-Jewish friends were accepted, but my application was lost three times running. I was finally informed by a sympathetic air corps officer that the air corps didn't want Jews." The young man then "pulled strings" to get a commission in the army.

 Learn It'n The **draft** is the selection of people for required military service.

A Prayer for Our Soldiers

A prayer that was jointly agreed upon by the different movements stated: "We beseech Thee, O God, to shield and protect our armed forces, in the air, on sea, and on land. May it be Thy will that the dominion of tyranny and cruelty speedily be brought to an end and the kingdom of righteousness be established on earth with liberty and freedom for all mankind." [from Jonathan D. Sarna, *American Judaism: A History* (New Haven: Yale University Press, 2004)]

Soldiers participate in a seder in 1943.

The Four Chaplains

The story of the sinking of the *USS Dorchester* in 1943 is a testament to interfaith cooperation. According to the story, the ship's four chaplains—two Protestants, a Catholic, and a Jew—gave their gloves and life belts to evacuating seamen and stood "arm and arm in prayer" as the torpedoed ship went down. [from Jonathan D. Sarna, *American Judaism: A History* [New Haven: Yale University Press, 2004]]

Do It
Design a postage stamp promoting interfaith understanding.

Look At It

This 1948 postage stamp depicts the chaplains and the words "Interfaith in Action."

Do It
Find other examples of prayers for the military. Write a prayer of your own for Jewish military personnel who are serving our country today.

Some Jews who had grown up in mostly urban Jewish neighborhoods were sent for training at bases located in the South and West. They were suddenly exposed to soldiers from parts of the country where Jews were a small minority of the population. One soldier from Brooklyn wrote, "I was in a strange land among people who hardly spoke my own language. On this foreign soil one could not find lox or bagels or **pumpernickel**. Here Southern fried chicken and grits were the popular delicacies."

Learn It

Pumpernickel is a type of dark rye bread.

Grits are coarsely ground and cooked grain.

Jewish soldiers also faced the irony of having to fight Nazi antisemitism while enduring their fellow soldiers' ethnic slurs. One serviceman recalled that the first time he was labeled a Jew or called an offensive name was in the army. Another remembered many incidents and "statements about our cowardice and Jewish unwillingness to fight. . . . Here we were fighting the Nazis, and then this madness in the United States Army! We are either despised,

A helmet issued to a Jewish chaplain.

EUROPE DURING SECOND WORLD WAR

Look At It

Legend:
- City or Town
- ⊕ National Capital
- - - National Boundaries
- Neutral Countries
- Axis Controlled (Max. Extent)
- Axis
- Allies

Do It

List the countries who fought with Germany (Axis) and those that fought against Germany (Allies).

mocked, or magnanimously tolerated." Jewish soldiers also faced a decision about whether they wanted an 'H,' for Hebrew, stamped on their identification tags.

In response to the antisemitism experienced by Jewish soldiers and civilians alike, liberal Jews and Christians joined together to promote better understanding and goodwill. This effort had begun in the 1920s with the founding of interfaith organizations such as the National Conference of Christians

and Jews, now known as The National Conference for Community and Justice (NCCJ). During the years between the two World Wars, a minister, a priest, and a rabbi—representatives of America's "three great faiths"—traveled the country together in an effort to confront religious prejudice. The term "Judeo-Christian" came to symbolize the idea that Western values arise from a shared religious consensus. The military, eager to promote religious harmony, encouraged Jewish, Catholic, and Protestant chaplains to participate together in goodwill meetings. At funerals for unidentified soldiers, three chaplains stood together at the grave of every unknown soldier and recited a similar burial service in English, Latin, and Hebrew.

AFTER THE WAR

After the collapse of the Third Reich, Europe was filled with **displaced** persons (DPs). They needed shelter, among other things, and American General Dwight Eisenhower ordered that Jewish DPs be housed in barracks with people from their European homelands—the very people who had cooperated with the Germans in murdering Jews. When news of this situation reached President Harry Truman, he directed Eisenhower to get the Jews out of the camps.

Jewish resettlement to free, democratic countries such as the U.S. or Great Britain still appeared uncertain. The Truman administration was not willing, at first, to change the immigration quotas. The leadership of the Hebrew Immigrant Aid Society and the American Jewish Committee petitioned Congress to liberalize the laws. Congress finally passed a Displaced Persons Act in 1950, and seven years after the end of the war in Europe, some 137,450 Jews had arrived in the United States, most of them DPs or survivors. The largest number of Jewish survivors settled in Israel or remained in Europe. [from Leonard Dinnerstein, *America and the Survivors of the Holocaust* (New York: Columbia University Press, 1986)]

In response to the destruction of European Jewry and antisemitism at home, the American Jewish community began to re-embrace Jewish life. Jewish leaders resolved to maintain Judaism in the face of opposition and danger, and to prepare the community to assume its role as the leader of worldwide Judaism. The *American Jewish Yearbook* reported in 1941 that, "American Jews are realizing that they have been spared for a sacred task— to preserve Judaism and its cultural, social, and moral values." Historian Jacob Rader Marcus declared, "The burden is solely ours to carry. Jewish culture and civilization and leadership are shifting rapidly to these shores." [from Jonathan D. Sarna, *American Judaism: A History* (New Haven: Yale University Press, 2004)]

Displaced means homeless.

As an American Jew, what is your responsibility to the future of the Jewish people in America and throughout the world?

UNIT 1 TIME LINE OF HISTORICAL EVENTS:
AMERICAN JEWS ENTER THE TWENTIETH CENTURY

| 1915 | 1920 | 1925 | 1930 | 1935 | 1940 | 1945 | 1950 | 1955 |

AMERICA

1920: A census reveals that the U.S. population has surpassed 100 million; Henry Ford's Model-T car accounts for more than half the cars sold in the U.S.

1931: "The Star-Spangled Banner" becomes the national anthem.

1947: Jackie Robinson joins the Brooklyn Dodgers as the first African American in baseball's major leagues.

1938: *Snow White and the Seven Dwarfs* is Disney's first full-length, animated film.

1950: The U.S. sends troops to aid South Korea in the Korean War.

1927: The first transatlantic phone is installed (3 minutes from London to New York costs $75); Babe Ruth hits 60 home runs and sets a baseball record.

1953: Tercentenary celebration (300th year) of Jews arriving in North America.

1954: Spies Julius and Ethel Rosenberg, convicted of selling secrets to the Soviet Union, are executed.

JEWISH AMERICA

1915: Moses Alexander is elected as the governor of Idaho, becoming the first Jewish governor.

1933: Stephen Wise and the American Jewish Congress declare a boycott on all German goods to protest the Nazi persecution of Jews.

1943: Hundreds of Orthodox Rabbis march in Washington, D.C., to promote support of rescue efforts to save European Jews.

1918: The American Jewish Congress is organized.

1939: Jewish songwriter Irving Berlin introduces his song, "God Bless America."

1948: Brandeis University, the only Jewish sponsored non-religious university, is founded.

1923: The first Hillel is started at the University of Illinois.

JEWISH WORLD

1919: The Third Aliyah begins, and lasts until 1923.

1932: The first Maccabiah Games (Jewish Olympics) are held; Jews from 14 countries participate.

1946: The Nuremberg Trials convict Nazis of persecuting the Jews during the Holocaust.

1922: The British are granted the mandate for Palestine by the League of Nations.

1947: The Dead Sea Scrolls are discovered in caves at Qumran, near the Dead Sea.

1924: The Fourth Aliyah begins, and lasts until 1928.

1935: The first woman rabbi, Regina Jonas, is privately ordained in Germany under the direction of the Reform movement.

1943: The Jews of the Warsaw Ghetto organized armed resistance against the Nazis in the Warsaw Ghetto Uprising.

1948: Israel declares its independence.

1929: The Fifth Aliyah begins, coming from Germany, and lasts until 1938.

1950: Israel declares Jerusalem as the capital of Israel; the Law of Return is enacted.

1914: Russian forces in retreat drive 600,000 Jews from their homes.

CHAPTER 4

BUILDING THE AMERICAN JEWISH COMMUNITY

What were some of the ways in which Jews moved into mainstream America in the postwar period?

In the years following World War II and the destruction of the European Jewish community, the United States became the center of world Judaism. The Jewish community had been growing in both size and strength, and many people were turning back toward religion. Judaism was now recognized as one of the country's three major religions, alongside Protestantism and Catholicism. The postwar period was a time of prosperity in the country as a whole and of building new institutions in the Jewish community. It was time for Jews to move into the mainstream of American life.

LINGERING FEAR AND PREJUDICE

Although the United States was victorious in World War II, the horrors of the war left Americans with the fear that other dictators might follow Hitler's example in seeking world **domination** and threatening the freedoms that Americans held dear. While the Soviet Union's Josef Stalin had been an ally during the war, there was now a great fear of Communism spreading throughout the world.

There was also a great fear of **subversion** because Communism had followers in the United States. At one time or another in the years following World War I, thousands of Americans, including many Jews, belonged to the Communist Party or were sympathetic to what they felt were its idealistic purposes. Official efforts to identify Communist spies and sympathizers began in 1947 when President Truman instituted a loyalty program within the federal government to identify Soviet **infiltrators**. The fear of Communism grew when the Soviet Union, with the assistance of spies in the U.S. like Julius and Ethel Rosenberg, joined the United States as a nuclear power, successfully testing a nuclear weapon for the first time in 1949.

Domination means "control."

Subversion is an underhanded way to overthrow an established authority.

Infiltrators are those who become part of an organization secretly.

Should the United States government have the right to demand loyalty from those who choose to work in government service, or do you think that this is an issue of personal freedom?

Congressman John Rankin, a Mississippi Democrat, blamed Jews for his losses in campaigns for Speaker of the House and House Democratic floor leader. As the Seventy-ninth Congress convened in January 1945, he proposed reviving a committee that had been **dormant** during the war years, the House Special Committee on Un-American Activities. Rankin announced his intention "to expose those elements that are insidiously trying to spread subversive propaganda, poison the minds of your children, distort the history of our country and discredit

How "A Star Is Born"
Ask The Hollywood Jew Who Owns One
BOYCOTT
The Jewish Boycotters

BOYCOTT
Every motion picture starring any member
of the
Pro-Communist Hollywood Anti-Nazi League
Destroy Jew Monopoly of the Motion
Picture Industry with its Sex Filth Films
and Jew-Communist Propaganda

One example of an antisemitic poster

Christianity." Rankin, therefore, decided to investigate the film industry.

Open hearings began in Washington, D.C., in October 1947. Members of the conservative Motion Picture Alliance for the Preservation of American Ideals testified to Communist activity in the Screen Writers and Screen Actors Guilds. Most of those who were named as Communists were Jews. When a group of Hollywood figures signed a petition opposing the congressional investigation, Congressman Rankin announced their names, emphasizing those who were Jewish.

The country's top film executives, almost all of whom were Jewish, dismissed those who had been called as witnesses because they had "impaired their usefulness to the industry." Although the alleged Communists had not been convicted of anything, the executives decided that these people would not be rehired until they had been acquitted or had declared under oath that they were not Communists. The decision, which denied work to any actor, writer, or director who fell under the least trace of

suspicion, was the beginning of the notorious "**blacklist**." Others felt they needed to "name names" of Communists or Communist sympathizers in the **Cold War** underway between the forces of western democracy and the Soviet empire. Those who named names sometimes endured harassment and loss of work.

Dormant means "inactive."

A **blacklist** is a list of people or organizations who are under suspicion or disfavor.

The **Cold War** is the struggle against expansionist Soviet Communism.

Why did these Jewish film executives decide not to rehire the alleged Communists?

One of the most well-known and outspoken advocates of the hunt for subversive Communists was Joseph McCarthy, a Republican from Wisconsin who was elected to the Senate in 1946. While McCarthy often claimed to have a list of Communists within the State Department, he never released the list, and the number of names it contained seemed to change with every speech. McCarthy led a wave of hearings in which

The Fifth Amendment and the Jewish View on Self-Incrimination

The Fifth Amendment to the U.S. Constitution was ratified in 1791 as part of the Bill of Rights. It states that no one may be forced to testify as a witness against himself or herself. In a *beit din* [Jewish court], defendants are prohibited from testifying against themselves (*Mishneh Sanhedrin* 9b). They are, however, allowed to make an argument for themselves.

Why do you think the *beit din* took this position? Why is this right important?

suspects had to answer the question, "Are you now or have you ever been a member of the Communist Party?"

Many of those called to testify before the senator's committee took the Fifth Amendment to avoid incriminating themselves, and they were then blacklisted from jobs in the movie industry. Other witnesses, however, were intimidated into acknowledging their own involvement and producing the names of colleagues and friends.

One specific case drew unwelcome attention to some Jews' ties to the Soviet Union, and other Jews feared that it might cause renewed antisemitism. Julius and Ethel Rosenberg were arrested in 1950 on suspicion of delivering secrets about the atomic bomb to the Soviet Union. Ethel Rosenberg's brother, David Greenglass, was assigned to the top-secret "Manhattan Project," which had created the bomb. He and Julius worked with a messenger to deliver Greenglass's sketches of key bomb parts to Soviet intermediaries. The Rosenbergs were convicted of conspiracy and sentenced to death; both were executed in 1953. Greenglass, who had testified against them, received a fifteen-year sentence. The Rosenbergs and Greenglass were Jewish, but as it turned out, antisemitism was not an issue since the judge, prosecutor, and defense attorneys were also Jewish. Fear of stirring up antisemitism, however, was very likely accountable for the harsh sentences they received.

Although some groups sought **clemency** for the Rosenbergs, especially since they had two young sons, the American Jewish Committee endorsed the death penalty. There was debate within the Jewish community over defending people accused of being Communists or aiding the Soviet Union. Fearing antisemitism, the American Jewish Committee established a panel to destroy the stereotype of the "Jewish Communist." It tried to uncover how Communists infiltrated Jewish organizations, and urged people to oppose organizations that represented Communist interests. The American Jewish Congress forcefully expelled its Communist members while, at the same time, opposing McCarthyism's attack on American civil liberties.

McCarthyism officially ended in 1954, after the public and press saw the senator's tactics firsthand during televised hearings. Public opinion turned against him, and the U.S. Senate investigated and then **censured** McCarthy for his behavior. Several months earlier, a Gallup Poll had shown that 65 percent of Jews opposed his search for Communists. McCarthy had never actually attacked Jews as a group; in fact, his two top aides were Jews.

Clemency means "mercy" or "leniency."

To **censure** is to express strong disapproval or criticism.

What were the dangers of McCarthyism to the Jewish community? What were the dangers to the United States?

POSTWAR PROSPERITY

Despite the brief period of McCarthyism, the years following World War II have been called a "golden age" for America's Jews. Religion in general enjoyed a revival, perhaps as a reaction to the horrors of the war and the threat of "godless Communism." Congress added the words "under God" to the Pledge of Allegiance in 1954; two years later, it made the phrase "In God We Trust," found on coins since the Civil War, the nation's official

Julius and Ethel Rosenberg

motto. Antisemites found themselves in an increasingly tolerant America. The 1950 *American Jewish Year Book* reported that "organized antisemitic activity, which began to decline after the war, continued only at a low level."

Federal and state legislation, pressure from returning veterans seeking jobs, government and media exposure, and the stigma of being compared to the Nazis ended much of the discrimination against Jews in employment, housing, and daily life. Court rulings led to the elimination of quotas that had kept Jewish students from entering certain colleges and universities. Some state legislatures made job discrimination illegal, and veterans groups opposed antisemitism. The number of Jews employed in blue-collar jobs declined. American Jews experienced unprecedented prosperity as they entered professions where they formerly were not hired, such as law and medicine. One study found an increase in the number of Jewish journalists, authors, engineers, architects, and college teachers. Large businesses increased their hiring of Jews, often in the very industries that had not previously welcomed them, such as auto manufacturing, insurance, and commercial banking. Most Jews had become middle class.

Wealthy Jews built on their previous successes in fields where they had traditionally been strong, including

Do It

There has been controversy over the words "under God" in the Pledge of Allegiance since they were added to the Pledge in 1954. The phrase was challenged in a case before the Supreme Court as recently as 2004. Where do Jewish organizations, such as the Jewish Community Relations Council or the American Jewish Committee, stand on this issue? What is your opinion? Write a letter to the editor or prepare to debate the issue.

The 1956 St. Louis ceremony dedicating a plaque and memorial to the 300th anniversary of the landing of Jews in America.

THE MISSOURI AMERICAN JEWISH TERCENTENARY SERVICE COMMEMORATING THE THREE HUNDREDTH ANNIVERSARY OF THE FIRST JEWISH SETTLEMENT IN THE UNITED STATES WAS HELD HERE ON SEPTEMBER 19, 1954.

The 300th Anniversary

In 1954, the American Jewish community celebrated the 300th anniversary of the first permanent Jewish community in North America. The theme of the celebration was "Man's Opportunities and Responsibilities under Freedom." President Dwight Eisenhower was guest of honor and keynote speaker at the opening event. Exhibitions, concerts, pageants, and public dinners took place in at least 400 cities around the country. The Jewish Museum in New York and the Smithsonian Institution in Washington, D.C. showed a national historical exhibition on the theme "Under Freedom." The National Symphony was commissioned and premiered a symphony entitled *Ahavah*. Eisenhower's address and other major events received national television coverage, and CBS and NBC broadcast specials on the American Jewish experience. Various national Jewish organizations published educational material for use in schools and adult education groups. [from Arthur A. Goren, "A 'Golden Decade' for American Jews: 1945–1955," in Jonathan D. Sarna, ed., *The American Jewish Experience* (New York: Holmes & Meier, 1997)]

Think About It

What was the importance of such a major celebration for the American Jewish community of the time? What celebrations are you aware of for the 350th anniversary that took place in 2004? What was their importance in America today?

Do It

Plan a poster celebrating the 400th anniversary of the Jews' arrival in America.

investment banking and department-store marketing. Jews owned the nation's leading newspapers, including *The New York Times* and *The Washington Post*, and continued to have an immense impact on broadcasting in America. William Paley, who had founded the Columbia Broadcasting System (CBS) in 1928, enjoyed continued success, as did Leonard Goldenson, the chairman of the American Broadcasting System (ABC). David Sarnoff became head of the Radio Corporation of America (RCA) in 1919, and his company profited from radio manufacturing, advertising, and patents for radio technology. Sarnoff began to focus his attention on television in 1933, and the first RCA televisions were produced in 1945.

As Jews became more financially comfortable and more socially secure, they began to follow other affluent Americans leaving the East Coast cities for the warmer Sunbelt states of the South and West. After the experience of being stationed in the South and West during the war, some Jewish men were interested in relocating there. As new industries and a strong job market grew, these areas became attractive to many Jews, who still preferred to live near other Jews in cities or their suburbs, rather than in rural areas. In fact, thousands of Jews chose two urban areas in particular—Miami and Los Angeles.

Many Jews moved out of the cities to the suburbs. Some settled in areas where most of their neighbors were not Jewish. Neighborhoods that had once refused entry to Jews now opened their doors to wealthier members of the Jewish community. This raised a fear, described by Jewish author Herman Wouk, that suburbanization carried "the threat of [Jews] pleasantly vanishing down a broad highway at the wheel of a high-powered station wagon, with the golf clubs piled in the back." [from Herman Wouk, *This Is My God*, (Garden City, New York: Doubleday, 1951)].

Others, mostly young families, found themselves living together in communities that were primarily Jewish. One of the most innovative planners of these suburban communities was William L. Levitt, who mass-produced homes, constructing thousands of inexpensive models. So-called "Levittowns" popped up outside several major cities; the most famous was on New York's Long Island, with some 17,000 homes.

 Think About It

What is your opinion of the fear expressed by Herman Wouk?

THE IMPORTANCE OF BELONGING

Despite the concern expressed by Wouk and others —that Jews would disappear in this new environment— synagogue membership became an important symbol of identity to Jews living in the suburbs. In 1949 and 1950, according to the *American Jewish Year Book*, "synagogue building continued," and "membership in synagogues and **affiliated** associations was on the increase." Forty percent of Jews belonged to synagogues, and by the late 1950s, that figure would reach 60 percent. As was reported to one researcher, "Judaism has changed. Nowadays people enjoy religion and going to synagogue." [from Jonathan D. Sarna, *American Judaism: A History* (New Haven: Yale University Press, 2004)]

 Learn It

Affiliated means "having a close association with another entity."

The newer synagogues, which tended to be Conservative or Reform, included space for recreational and educational activities. They were often luxurious, reflecting the pride the members felt in their religion and the importance of the synagogue as a symbol of Jewish culture in the suburbs. Many Jews joined only after they had children, wanting the children to have a sense of Jewish identity through the marking of life-cycle events such as births, *b'nei mitzvah*, weddings, and funerals. Practices such as lighting Hanukkah and Shabbat candles, holding a Passover seder, and celebrating the High Holidays were generally maintained, but observing dietary laws and Shabbat restrictions often were not.

Do It

Do you live in the city, suburbs, a small town, or a rural area? Are there many Jews in your community? Are there many synagogues and Jewish agencies and organizations? Write a brief description of your Jewish community, including what you like and dislike about it. In your opinion, what would make an ideal Jewish community?

_____

_____

_____

_____

_____

_____

_____

_____

Members felt pride in the Moses Montefiore Temple in Bloomington, Illinois.

Think About It What does your Jewish identity mean to you? What makes you feel Jewish?

The Reform movement grew dramatically between 1937 and 1957; membership climbed from 50,000 families to 255,000. The movement's seminaries —the Jewish Institute of Religion in New York City and the Hebrew Union College in Cincinnati—merged in 1950 to form one school with separate campuses and faculties. The Union of American Hebrew Congregations (UAHC), now known as the Union of Reform Judaism (URJ), appointed Rabbi Maurice Eisendrath president in 1946, and he challenged the movement to make changes that would attract the suburbanites to Reform Judaism.

Reform leaders and congregational members placed greater emphasis on Hebrew language, Zionism and the new State of Israel, and the newly popular bat mitzvah ceremony. The role of women expanded in the Reform movement, as did their participation in social action. Rabbi Eisendrath stressed issues such as world peace and civil rights, declaring that "the heart of religion concerns itself with man's relation to man." While some Reform Jews opposed them, such innovations were, for the most part, quite popular and attracted many new members to Reform congregations.

During the same period, the Conservative movement increased from approximately 75,000 members to more than 200,000. The movement saw itself as the "centrist" movement—between Orthodoxy and Reform—and made changes that appealed to the newly suburbanized Jews. One decision permitted limited use of electricity on Shabbat for such activities as turning on lights and using the telephone, radio and television. And, because Conservative leaders believed that living in widely spread-out suburbs might make observance more difficult, they agreed in 1950 that members could drive their cars on Shabbat for the sole purpose of attending services.

This was a radical departure from tradition, and one that the Orthodox refused to make. Because of the biblical prohibition on traveling, Orthodox congregations sprang up in areas where people could walk to services. Members then encouraged the development of businesses that catered to their specific religious needs, such as kosher butchers, bakeries, and restaurants. Orthodoxy, however, was losing ground during these years. While the number of Orthodox did fall far below the number of Conservative and Reform Jews, the movement was sustained by the knowledge and commitment of its members.

The role of women in the synagogue became an increasingly important issue within the Reform and Conservative movements. Conservative synagogues began to call women to the Torah for a group *aliyah* on Simhat Torah. In 1954, the Conservative Rabbinical Assembly favored measures "leading to the complete equalization of the status of women in Jewish law." One year later, the Committee on Jewish Law and Standards permitted women to be called to the Torah on a regular basis.

Beginning with rabbis sympathetic to Reconstructionism and spreading gradually through the Conservative movement, the bat mitzvah became more popular. By the early 1950s, more than half of Conservative synagogues offered girls this life-cycle ritual.

Most girls chanted the *haftarah*, although some also read from the Torah. Within the Reform movement in the early 1960s, women active in the National Federation of Temple Sisterhoods began asking that women be ordained as rabbis. Girls were becoming more active in youth activities, young women were attending Hebrew Union College undergraduate classes, and a few began to think about the possibility of becoming rabbis.

 The *haftarah* is the weekly portion read from the Prophets, following the Torah reading.

What is your opinion of these changes in the status of women and girls in Jewish religious life?

TEACH IT DILIGENTLY

Jewish education blossomed during this period. The number of children receiving a Jewish education more than doubled between 1948 and 1958, and in 1959 the American Association for Jewish Education estimated that "more than 80 percent of Jewish children attended one or another type of Jewish school during . . . their elementary

Young Jewish women at a confirmation in Flushing, Queens in 1948

school years." **Allocations** to Jewish schools from Jewish philanthropies tripled between 1943 and 1959, an indication of the community's interest in education.

Allocations are money that is set aside for a specific purpose.

Conservative synagogues led the way, but Reform and Orthodox synagogues followed their example. Because many Jewish children outside the Orthodox community attended public schools, afternoon Hebrew schools and Sunday schools played a central role in Jewish education. Interest in Jewish day schools also grew, with the number of students jumping from 14,000 at the end of World War II to 62,000 in 1967. While the vast majority were in New York City, day schools eventually existed in thirty-three states.

At first, day schools were sponsored only by the Orthodox movement. In 1944, Rabbi Shraga Feivel Mendlowitz founded Torah Umesorah, the National Society for Hebrew Day Schools, with the goal of establishing a day school in every community. In 1958, the Conservative movement opened the Solomon Schechter schools. With their dual secular and Judaic curricula, Jewish day schools provided a quality education that was comparable to the best public schools.

Reinforcing Jewish identity through means other than school programs gained in popularity at this time. As long ago as 1909, with the formation of Young Judaea, youth groups helped to involve teens in their heritage through social and educational programs. The National Federation of Temple Youth (NFTY), which was founded in 1939 as a way for young people to become involved in the life of their Reform synagogues, grew during this period, lowered its membership age from college to high school, and held its first educational overnight summer camp at a newly purchased facility in Wisconsin. The Conservative movement founded its Ramah camps in 1947, and also founded United Synagogue Youth (USY), a youth group for teens from thirteen to seventeen, in 1951. The National Conference of Synagogue Youth (NCSY), an Orthodox youth group interested in outreach

Speaking about Day School

What is the value of day school? An Orthodox Jewish educator wrote a rationale for this type of education:

Look At It

. . . Exposed to both disciplines [Judaic and General Studies] in a congenial environment, the child learns to integrate the traditional with the modern, the secular with the religious, his Jewish heritage with American civilization. . . . he learns to be a good American Jew. He learns that to be a good Jew is to be a good American. . . .

[from Alvin Irwin Schiff, "The Value of a Jewish Day School Education," in Jacob Rader Marcus, ed., *The Jew in the American World: A Source Book* (Detroit: Wayne State University Press, 1996)]

Think About It

Whether or not you attend Jewish day school, what do you see as the advantages or the disadvantages of this type of education?

Do It

Interview someone who has attended a Jewish camp or belonged to a Jewish youth group. How did the experience affect the person's Jewish identity and relationship to the Jewish community?

Archery practice at a Jewish summer camp

to unaffiliated Jewish youth, also dates from the 1950s. In the years since then many youth groups and camps were founded; for example, the Jewish Reconstructionist Federation founded a youth group in the 1990s and its Camp JRF in 2002.

Jewish higher education also underwent big changes during this period. After the war, YIVO, the Institute for Jewish Research, received thousands of books and manuscripts stolen by the Nazis, greatly enlarging its library. The YIVO's Vilna branch moved to New York during World War II and played a major role in the city's Jewish intellectual life, providing courses and lectures in Yiddish and Jewish history, publishing books and pamphlets, and offering researchers access to a collection of rare manuscripts and publications. Brandeis University, the first Jewish-sponsored, secular university in the United States, opened in suburban Boston in 1948. The university, built with contributions from wealthy Jews, attracted many of the finest Jewish scholars to its faculty. Its first president, Abram L. Sachar, called it "a corporate gift of Jews to higher education."

BUILDING COMMUNITY

The postwar period saw the arrival of significant numbers of immigrants, including some of Judaism's most prominent scholars. Many lived in their own communities, and wanted to rebuild the society they had lost. The most visible of these immigrants were members of Hasidic groups that settled in Brooklyn, establishing more than twenty-five communities, each loyal to its own *rebbe*.

 Rebbe is the Yiddish word for the rabbi-leader of a Hasidic group.

Traditional in belief, most isolated themselves from the secular world and introduced dancing, singing, and swaying into their prayer services. Some, such as the Satmar (the name of the city in Hungary where they originated)—even set up a village of their own in New York State. The Lubavitch, originally from Belarus in Eastern Europe, were followers of Rabbi Joseph I. Schneersohn, and then of his son-in-law and distant cousin, Rabbi Menahem Mendel Schneerson, known as the Rebbe. The Lubavitch are dedicated to "wisdom, understanding, and knowledge" —the Hebrew **acronym** for which is Chabad, a name by which they also came to be known. Unlike other Hasidic groups, they reached out to affiliated and unaffiliated Jews, hoping to help them strengthen their religious consciousness. Known for their deep belief in the power of Jews' efforts to bring the messiah through observing mitzvot, they planned large public events such as Hanukkah candle-lighting ceremonies. Personal emissaries, called *shluchim*, were sent by the Rebbe to set up institutions around the world to promote a Hasidic Orthodox lifestyle.

 An **acronym** is a word formed from the first letters of words in a phrase.

 Have you ever seen or experienced a public Lubavitch ceremony such as a candle-lighting? Some Jews feel that religious observances should be kept in the home and synagogue. What is your opinion?

As Jews enjoyed the benefits of the postwar economic growth, the achievements of some individuals made them feel more a part of American life. Just a few weeks after the end of the war, Bess Myerson was crowned the first Jewish Miss America. Many American Jews were particularly

One of the Lubavitch outreach activities

proud because she was the daughter of working-class immigrants who spoke Yiddish at home. Most important, she rejected a suggestion from pageant officials that she compete under a less obviously Jewish name.

Laura Z. Hobson's best-selling novel, *Gentleman's Agreement*, which was made into an Oscar-winning film in 1947, has been credited with raising public awareness of stereotypes and changing attitudes toward Jews. The story recounts the experiences of Phil Green, a gentile reporter who pretends to be Jewish for eight weeks to record how he is treated. Green falls in love with a woman and finds that she exhibits subtle forms of antisemitism. In one scene, Green says, "You can be an American and a Protestant, Catholic, or a Jew. Religion is different from nationality."

The famous author, Elie Wiesel, now a U.S. citizen, has dedicated his life to making sure that the world remembers what happened to the Jews during the Holocaust and fighting prejudice wherever it appears. A survivor of the Nazi death camp, Auschwitz, he stated that, "To remain silent and indifferent is the greatest sin of all." He broke a vow to remain silent about his experiences with the publication of his first and most famous book, *Night,* in 1958. He wrote, "Never shall I forget that night, the first night in camp, which has turned my life into one long night. . . . Never shall I forget the little faces of the children. . . . Never shall I forget that **nocturnal** silence which deprived me, for all eternity, of the desire to live. . . ." In recognition of his work, he won the Nobel Peace Prize in 1986.

Nocturnal means "occurring in the night."

There were many other well-known Jews—authors, sports greats, entertainers, politicians, as well as great Jewish thinkers and philosophers—who made contributions to American life during the postwar years. Although the beginning of the era was marked by lingering fear and prejudice, it became a golden time for American Jews who were building their lives in the "*goldeneh medinah*."

Bess Myerson would soon become Miss America.

Elie Wiesel wrote a piece that was published in *The New York Times* (Sunday, September 27, 1992) in which he stated:

"I still believe that to be Jewish today means what it meant yesterday and a thousand years ago. It means for the Jew in me to seek fulfillment both as a Jew and as a human being. . . . To be Jewish today is to recognize that every person is created in the image of God and that our purpose in living is to be a reminder of God. . . . The mission of the Jewish people has never been to make the world more Jewish, but to make it more human."

Write an essay about what being Jewish means to you.

How has the relationship between American Jews and Israel grown and developed since the founding of the State?

A s soon as statehood was declared, on May 14, 1948, they danced the hora in the streets. But although American Jews, like Jews throughout the world, were elated at the founding of the Jewish state, the relationship between American and Israeli Jews began uneasily. American Jews supported the new nation financially and emotionally, but for the most part, they were not inclined to move there. Israeli Jews insisted that a true Zionist should move to Israel and that American Jews were still living in *galut* [exile]. Over the years, however, through wars and periods of relative peace, American Jews have continued to support *Medinat Yisrael* [the State of Israel].

EARLY SUPPORT FOR THE NEW COUNTRY

Initially, many American Jews, especially leaders of the American Jewish Committee, worried that loyalty to Israel might be interpreted as disloyalty to the United States. Tensions relaxed when Israel's first prime minister, David Ben-Gurion, met with Jacob Blaustein, president of the AJC, in 1950. Ben-Gurion issued a statement that, "the Jews of the United States, as a community and as individuals, have only one political attachment and that is to the United States of America." The agreement also stated that Israel respected the "integrity of Jewish life in the democratic countries," and fully accepted that "the Jews of the United States do not live 'in exile.'"

There is a traditional Jewish view that Jews living outside of the land of Israel are living in *galut* or "exile." What is your reaction to this?

While only about 1,000 moved to Israel between 1948 and 1951, American Jews showed their interest and concern in other ways. Many American Jewish philanthropists saw the new state as an ideal recipient of their gifts. Local federations gave more money than they had previously to the United Jewish Appeal (UJA), which in turn gave a larger

percentage to Israel. Henry Morgenthau, Jr., Roosevelt's former secretary of the treasury, headed this effort immediately after the war, and about 5.5 million American Jews made donations in 1948.

David Ben-Gurion made only one trip abroad during his initial term in office, and that was to the United States to launch the first Israel Bonds campaign in 1951. The sale of bonds, which supported the growing **infrastructure** of the country, fulfilled Ben-Gurion's dream of a strong economic partnership between Israel and its supporters around the world.

The **infrastructure** of a country includes its electricity, dams, water supply, roads, bridges, communications, and transportation facilities.

American money played an essential role in the nation's early survival as 700,000 penniless refugees from the war in Europe entered the country. The economy was weak, food and clothing were rationed, and the need to maintain a military reserve against the surrounding enemy nations made high taxes a necessity. Yet despite their financial support, many American Jews remained somewhat detached from Israel emotionally. A survey at the end of the 1950s showed that only forty-eight of more than 1,000 religious school educators reported teaching about Israel. Few American

Jews traveled to Israel in the 1950s.

Yet Israel did influence American Jewish life. Prayers for the State of Israel were regularly introduced in some synagogues, and the Israeli flag was often seen at Jewish events. Israeli products were sold in synagogue gift shops and American Jews owned objects made in Israel. Numerous educators switched from Ashkenazic to Sephardic Hebrew, as is used in Israel, and many American Jewish youth attended Zionist camps.

Do It

Find out whether anyone in your family has invested in Israel Bonds and why they felt it was important to do so. Create a poster or ads for bonds.

Learn It

Nationalize means to bring under the control or ownership of a nation.

A **concession** is something that is given up in political negotiations.

For information about AIPAC issues, to read press releases, and to read important speeches from Congressional leaders, administration officials, and Israeli leaders, click on http://www.aipac.org.

THE SINAI CAMPAIGN

Egypt closed the Suez Canal to Israeli shipping in 1949, refusing to comply with a United Nations Security Council order to reopen it. Egyptian President Gamal Abdel Nasser began increasing his arms supply from the Soviet Union, and in 1955 he announced, ". . . There will be no peace on Israel's border because we demand vengeance, and vengeance is Israel's death." *Fedayeen*, terrorists trained and equipped by Egypt and based mainly in Jordan, began attacking Israel, committing acts of sabotage and murder. The U.N. Security Council condemned only Israel's counterattacks.

Nasser next blockaded the Strait of Tiran and **nationalized** the canal, in July 1956. Faced with increased terrorist attacks and the blockade of Israeli shipping, and with the support of France and Britain, Israel attacked Egypt on October 29 and advanced to the canal. However, under heavy pressure from the Soviet Union and the United States, Israel withdrew from the Sinai without obtaining any **concessions** from Egypt. The United States guaranteed that the Strait of Tiran would remain open and sponsored a U.N. resolution to create the United Nations Emergency Force (UNEF) to supervise the territories that Israel evacuated. Angry that Israel had gone to war without U.S. approval, Eisenhower still held out the threat of punishment for Israel. The Conference of Presidents of Major American Jewish Organizations, an umbrella group representing major Jewish groups, argued that as an ally of the United States, Israel deserved fair treatment and that the country served as a deterrent to Nasser's ambitions of expanding throughout the region. The job of conveying this message to government leaders fell to the American Israel Public Affairs Committee (AIPAC)

Despite the fact that AIPAC'S leader, I.L. Kenen, won support from congressional leaders who warned that they would oppose any actions imposing economic **sanctions** on Israel, Eisenhower made a televised address that vaguely threatened to discipline Israel. Two of Eisenhower's cabinet members also suggested that the federal government outlaw private donations to Israel, purchases of Israeli Bonds, and other gifts and investments. When Kenen found out, he roused opposition in Congress and the media and Eisenhower dropped the plan.

By the late 1950s, AIPAC, known as the "Jewish **lobby**," was expanding its staff, keeping detailed congressional voting records on issues involving the Middle East, and widening its contacts. It was able to influence Congress, although reaching understandings with the Eisenhower administration was difficult. Membership in AIPAC continued to grow under Kenen and his successors and by 1980, American Jews backed more than seventy **political action committees** that helped finance the campaigns of candidates sympathetic to Israel.

Learn It

Sanctions are punishing legal or economic actions by one nation toward another to force it to comply with legal, political, or humanitarian obligations.

A **lobby** is a group of private persons who attempt to influence the voting of lawmakers.

A **political action committee** is a committee formed by a corporation or organization to collect voluntary contributions to support candidates because the corporation is either limited by election campaign laws to only contributing a specified amount to a candidate or prohibited from giving money directly to the candidate.

ATTACHMENT TO ISRAEL GROWS

American Jews became more concerned about Israel in the 1960s, at the same time that heightened awareness of the Holocaust was growing. When the Israeli secret service captured and arrested Nazi leader Adolf Eichmann in Argentina in 1960, it intensified memories of the horrors of the Holocaust. As the Gestapo's expert on Jewry, Eichmann had had primary responsibility for sending millions of Jews to their deaths. He was taken to Israel, tried for his crimes, and executed in 1962. The case reawakened Jews to their vulnerability and unleashed a flood of books on the topic. Many of these books looked beyond the Germans to place some measure of blame for the Holocaust on victims who allegedly did not resist; on Pope Pius XII who was accused of indifference to Nazi cruelty; and on Franklin Roosevelt, who, it was claimed, did not act strongly or quickly enough to save European Jews. Eichmann's trial also made American Jews look at Israel in a new light.

Do It

Find out about lobbying efforts that support Israel today. What is your opinion of the value of these organizations?

Click on It

To read about the Eichmann trial, click on http://www.pbs.org/eichmann.

Adolf Eichmann on trial in Jerusalem

The popular film, *Exodus*, based on the Leon Uris novel of the same name, debuted in 1960. It contributed to both the image of Israelis as brave pioneers and the identification of American Jews and non-Jews with the State of Israel. Other movies, as well as books, television programs, and magazine articles, were sympathetic to Israel and helped Americans to see the nation positively. The United Jewish Appeal began actively training Jewish leaders to be proud of their Jewish identity and their connection to Israel. People toured Israel to increase their understanding of the country, and when these tours were called "missions" or "pilgrimages" they took on religious significance.

Support for Israel increased greatly as a result of the Six Day War, which also strengthened the identity of American Jews. In the spring of 1967,

From the Holocaust to the Birth of the Jewish State

Two new holidays on the Jewish calendar emphasized the connection between the Holocaust and the birth of the State of Israel. Yom HaShoah (Holocaust Memorial Day), established by Israel's parliament in 1951 and widely observed beginning in the 1970s, is a day of mourning and remembrance. Observed one week later, Yom Ha'Atzma'ut, Israel Independence Day, is a day of joy and thanksgiving. Prayer books link the holidays: "the rebirth of Israel from the ashes of the *Shoah* is a symbol of hope against despair, of redemption against devastation." (from the Reform movement's *Gates of the Seasons*). The "March of the Living," a teen Israel program, builds on this idea. Moving from a silent procession at the Auschwitz death camp to joyful visits to special sites in Israel, the March conveys the same message.

Do It

Design a ceremony for your school's commemoration of these two holidays.

Israel's neighbors again began making threats, and in June, Egypt again blockaded the Strait of Tiran and Arab armies gathered on Israel's borders. On June 5, Israel responded with a powerful attack that crushed Egypt's air power. Confronted with opposition from Jordan and Syria as well, Israel took control of the Gaza Strip and advanced into the Sinai Desert. When the fighting ended six days later, Israeli forces controlled the Sinai, Syria's Golan Heights, and all of Jordan's territory west of the Jordan River, including a now-unified Jerusalem, home of the Western Wall, Judaism's holiest site.

Americans show support for Israel at a fundraiser for Israel bonds.

American Jews were filled with pride and amazement at Israel's ability to defeat so many foes so quickly. Those who had not previously felt ties to Israel now considered Israel to be a key part of their Jewish identity. Public opinion polls found that ninety-nine out of 100 Jews strongly supported Israel. The American media treated the Israelis as heroes, triumphant despite incredible opposition, and American Jews connected with that image. They opened their wallets, as well as their hearts, to Israel.

Donations soared from $136 million in 1966 to $240 million in 1967. At one luncheon, $15 million was donated in fifteen minutes. One Holocaust survivor donated her life savings of $5,000 and some youth groups gave their entire treasuries to the United Jewish Appeal. The Jewish Theological Seminary, which had forbidden the playing of *Hatikvah* [the Israeli National Anthem] at its 1948 graduation, released a statement saying, "The people of Israel have the privilege to give their lives to preserve the very existence of the nation. The best we Jews in America can do is to support them with our money."

American Jews also stepped forward to volunteer for Israel, taking civilian jobs so that Israelis could fight. Israeli embassies and Hillel directors on American college campuses reported receiving a flood of calls. By the time the United

An American Volunteer's Story

One American volunteer described his experience during the war:

Look At It

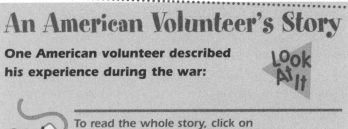

Click On It

To read the whole story, click on
http://www.wzo.org.il/en/resources/view

I had been assigned as leader of a group of civilian volunteers that would do the work of recovering the equipment.

. . . Many volunteers were . . . unconnected with the culture or with Israel, except for the fact that we were Jewish and we had felt something and came from all over the world. Spontaneous singing would be a common occurrence during the next months, helping build an emotional link among us, even though few understood the Hebrew. . . .

We were home, profoundly happy to be there, aware that volunteering meant something, undefined but life-changing. Our ancestors came from this land, two millennia ago. Our ancient homeland and culture beckoned, and we had returned.

States placed a ban on travel to the Middle East, 10,000 applications had been recorded. On the day prior to the outbreak of war, a New Yorker approached a Jewish Agency official saying, "I have no money to give, but here are my sons. Please send them over immediately."

Former American Jewish Congress president and historian Rabbi Arthur Hertzberg wrote that American Jews had come together "with deep Jewish commitments as they have never been united before." Rabbi Abraham Joshua Heschel, a professor of Jewish ethics and mysticism at the Jewish Theological Seminary of America and one of the most influential modern philosophers of religion among both Christians and Jews, commented that, "before the war, Jews went to pray for the survival of Israel, and afterwards, to give thanks." The war reenergized the American Jewish community, with many people showing a greater interest in Jewish spirituality and learning.

After the war, it became more common for American Jewish teens to spend a summer in Israel, and Israel became an increasingly important part of the curriculum of Jewish schools. Jewish tourism to Israel grew 100 percent in the first year after the war, and the number of Americans making *aliyah* grew more than 500 percent in the years immediately following the war. The war also led many Jews to become more involved in American politics, especially on issues relating to Israel and other Jewish causes. Just before the fighting began in 1967, nearly 150,000 supporters of Israel marched through the streets of New York in support of the Jewish state. Many organizations bombarded officials and the media with position papers and petitions. During the conflict, President Lyndon B. Johnson gave Israel unprecedented access to weapons and ordered the Sixth Fleet into the eastern Mediterranean to discourage the Soviet Union from attempting to aid the Arab nations.

Do It

Create a poem, song, dance, essay, sculpture, or picture that expresses your feelings about Israel and your connection to the ancient land and the modern nation.

Support of Israel was not universal, however. Jews involved in **ecumenical** organizations were shocked to witness Christian institutions' neutrality as the Arab nations confronted Israel. Although some Christian leaders spoke out individually in support of Israel, many Christian organizations, with whom they had worked on interfaith dialogue, seemed to focus more attention on the plight of Arab refugees than on the survival of Israel. Jewish leaders, however, made it clear that the continued existence of Israel was not open for debate. David Polish, a Reform rabbi, wrote in the *Christian Century* that as a result of Christians' "moral failure, the much **touted** Christian-Jewish dialogue is revealed as fragile and superficial."

Learn It

Ecumenical means "promoting religious unity throughout the world."

Tout means to "advertise" or to "foster interest."

YET ANOTHER WAR AND ITS AFTERMATH

In 1971, Egyptian President Anwar Sadat had offered the possibility that he might sign a peace agreement with Israel if the Israeli government would return the territories it had **annexed** after the Six Day War. Israel rejected Sadat's offer. Then, in 1973, Egypt and Syria attacked Israel on the holiest day in the Jewish calendar—Yom Kippur.

Learn It

Annex means to incorporate a state, territory, or country into another.

At first, Israel was outgunned and outmanned. At the border with Syria on the Golan Heights, 180 Israeli tanks faced 1,400 Syrian guns. Near the Suez Canal, 500 Israeli soldiers faced 80,000 Egyptians. Iraq, Saudi Arabia, Kuwait, Libya, Algeria, Tunisia, and Sudan provided the Arab forces with both money and men. Palestinian terrorists based in Lebanon attacked Israeli civilians. Jordan, apparently with some reluctance, sent two military units to assist the Arab forces. The Soviet Union resupplied the Arabs by air and sea.

President Richard Nixon's administration responded to the Soviet action by approving a huge airlift to deliver provisions for Israel's military and proposing that Congress allocate $2.2 billion to aid the Israeli defense efforts. The American Jewish response to this latest attack on Israel was heightened by outrage over the choice of Yom Kippur as the day for the initial assault, and the realization that the challenges Israel faced, both economically and militarily, were more difficult than those of 1967. As a result, more than 30,000 American Jews offered to go to Israel and work. The United Jewish Appeal collected $107 million in the war's first week alone.

The war ended in three weeks, after a United Nations Security Council resolution called for an end to the fighting. Although Israel had pushed Syrian forces back beyond the 1967 ceasefire line and had crossed the Suez Canal, claiming part of the west bank of Egypt, the war took the lives of 2,688 soldiers and put the nation in severe economic difficulty.

For the first time, the Arab nations used oil as a means to punish Israel's allies. An **embargo** on oil exports began in October 1973 and continued through May 1974. The British government declared a state of emergency, and there was gasoline rationing in the United States.

 Learn It An **embargo** is a legal restriction on trade with a foreign nation.

Ironically, Anwar Sadat later became a leading proponent of peace in the Middle East. He visited Jerusalem and met with Israeli leaders and, in 1979, he and Israeli Prime Minister Menachem Begin signed the Camp David Peace Accord.

This set up a framework for peace in the Middle East that included Israeli withdrawal from the Sinai. Sadat paid for his desire to make peace with Israel when Islamic fundamentalists assassinated him in 1981.

American Jews contributed to the campaigns of many U.S. politicians during this period, most

Do It Find the Suez Canal and the Strait of Tiran. Why were these areas so strategically important to Israel?

Look At It

Events leading to the Six Day War, 1967

— Egyptian blockade
☐ Israeli territory before Six Day War

Mediterranean Sea

May 19, 1967: UN forces withdraw from Sinai according to Egyptian demand.

Advance of Lebanese Army
Lebanon
Golan Heights
Advance of Syrian Army
Syria
Haifa
Samaria
Tel Aviv
Jaffa
Jerusalem
Advance of Iraqi Army
Judea
Gaza
Beer Sheba
El Arish
Suez Canal
Abu Aweigila
Advance of Egyptian Army
Advance of Jordanian Army
Jordan
Kuntilla
Sinai Peninsula
Ras Al-Nagb
Eilat
Gulf of Eilat
Advance of Saudi Arabian Army
Gulf of Suez
Egypt
0   40 km
0   40 mi
Sharm el Sheikh
Strait of Tiran
Red Sea
Saudi Arabia

Think About It
After examining the map of the movement of enemy troops prior to the Six Day War, what is your reaction to Israel's victory?

© 2005 Koret Communications Ltd. www.koret.com

Sadat and Begin shown with President Jimmy Carter after the signing of the Camp David Peace Accord

Ask a parent, teacher, rabbi, or an adult friend what they remember about any of Israel's wars. Tape record or write their answer.

The resolution against Zionism was finally repealed in late 1991, although even then, twenty-five nations maintained the position that Zionism represented racism. Israeli Foreign Minister David Levy said that the decision to repeal the resolution removed "a terrible stain" on the United Nations' record and the World Jewish Congress called the decision a "victory for decency."

Think About It — What does the existence of this resolution say to you about Israel's position in the United Nations?

of whom were Democrats. But in 1972, when the Democratic presidential candidate George McGovern failed to take a strong pro-Israel position, many Jews supported Republican Richard Nixon's re-election and Nixon won a landslide victory.

By the mid 1970s, leaders of Jewish federations had started to worry about the urgent needs at home that were not being met while large amounts of money went to Israel, and the number of contributions to the United Jewish Appeal campaigns decreased. From a high of $660 million in 1974 following the Yom Kippur War, donations declined to $475 million the next year and remained at that level for several years. The question became how to balance local needs with Israel's needs, especially as Israel's economy grew.

In 1975, the United Nations General Assembly overwhelmingly passed Resolution 3379, which stated that Zionism was "a form of racism and racial discrimination" threatening world peace and security. The resolution questioned Israel's right to exist and "called upon all countries to oppose this racist . . . ideology." After it was approved, the U.S. Ambassador to the United Nations Daniel P. Moynihan stated that the United States "does not acknowledge [the resolution], it will never abide, it will never acquiesce in this infamous act." For many years, the resolution allowed other nations to place a black mark against Israel and to annually attempt to oust Israel from the U.N.

In 1987, an American Jew, Jonathan Pollard, who worked as a civilian American naval intelligence analyst, pleaded guilty to passing classified American documents to the Israeli government. Pollard received a life sentence and his wife was sentenced to five years in prison for assisting him. The Conference of Presidents of Major American Jewish Organizations endorsed the life sentence. AIPAC leaders' fears that the Pollard case would incite new antisemitism did not come to pass, although some non-Jewish politicians did speak out publicly against the power of the American Jewish lobbying organizations. The case remains complicated and controversial.

ISRAEL AND NON-ORTHODOX JEWS

Since its founding, Israel has embraced Orthodox Judaism as the official religion of the state, despite the fact that most Israelis are secular. Conservative, Reform, and Reconstructionist Jews have experienced significant frustration in their efforts to achieve legal equality—and they have received support for those efforts from Jews in the United States. Moreover, of the 17,000 American Jews who immigrated to Israel between 1967 and 1973, about two-thirds returned to the United States.

In 1968, the World Union of Progressive Judaism, the international umbrella organization for the non-Orthodox movements, scheduled its convention in Jerusalem. Although the Israeli government greeted the group warmly, the Israeli rabbinate did not. The minister of religious affairs would not allow the group to conduct a planned Reform service, on the grounds that mixed seating would be inappropriate.

The question of conversion and who has the right to immigrate to Israel under the Law of Return has been particularly controversial. The law states that, "Every Jew has the right to come to this country as an *oleh*." A 1970 amendment specified that converts were permitted but did not spell out the type of conversion required. The religious parties in the Knesset have attempted to make the law apply only to Orthodox conversions, and the issue has yet to be decided.

 Oleh means a new immigrant to Israel. *Olah* is the feminine form.

 Should Israel have the right to make whatever laws it wants regarding who is considered a Jew for purposes of immigration or should worldwide Jewry have a say in matters of Jewish identity?

ADDITIONAL FRUSTRATIONS

American Jews had begun to criticize some of Israel's policies as early as the 1960s. When Israel invaded Lebanon in 1982, Israeli public opinion was mixed, as were reactions in the American Jewish community.

Arabs in Palestine still did not accept the existence of Israel, and in the 1980s and 1990s many resorted to violence. The *Intifada*, a series of demonstrations, strikes, riots, and violence, began in the Gaza Strip in 1987. It was notable both for the amount of popular participation and the part played by Islamic groups who advocated the creation of an Islamic state. Such a state would include all of historic Palestine, an area encompassing Israel. In 1988, one of the groups, Yasser Arafat's Palestine Liberation Organization (PLO) began supporting the establishment of a Palestinian state coexisting with Israel. It did not, however, forgo violence.

In 1993 and 1995, agreements between the PLO and Israel, with the support of the United States, established Palestinian control over the Gaza Strip and portions of the West Bank. Israeli Prime Minister Yitzhak Rabin was assassinated in 1995 at a peace rally in Tel Aviv for his role in the peace effort. He had indicated his willingness to give up Israeli-occupied territory in order to make peace with Israel's Arab neighbors. Over the years, the drive for peace faltered as Israelis became increasingly discouraged by Arafat's failure to renounce terrorist attacks on Israeli civilians. In the wake of Arafat's death in November 2004, new leadership continues to work on the peace process, but most experts predict years of turmoil while a new Palestinian order emerges.

 Do research on the *Intifada*, the PLO, Anwar Sadat, Yasser Arafat, or Yitzhak Rabin.

THE *MATZAV*

Matzav is the Hebrew word for "situation," which is how Israelis refer to the latest violent rebellion by Palestinians against Israel, begun in 2000. This campaign, both before and since 2000, has included suicide bombings of civilians in Israel, making everyday life uneasy. In an effort to prevent the infiltration into Israel by Palestinian terrorists, Israel began constructing a wall to separate Israel from the West Bank in 2001. While American Jews have been horrified by the deaths of innocent Israeli victims, some have voiced displeasure with Israeli policies.

Whatever their views on Israeli politics, most American Jews think of Israel as a Jewish spiritual homeland and support the continued existence of the Jewish state.

 Is the nation of Israel important to you as an American Jew? Why or why not?

CHAPTER 6

MENDING THE WORLD

In what ways did Jews become involved in actions to achieve social reform in the general community? Why were many Jews drawn to these activities?

Perhaps Hillel said it best: "If I am not for myself, who will be for me? If I am only for myself, what am I? And if not now, when? (Pirkei Avot 1:14) In the years following World War II, Jews in the United States took this teaching to heart. They looked outside the Jewish community and saw problems that needed solutions, realized that they now had the money and influence to make a difference, and asked themselves, "If not us, who?" and "If not now, when?"

What do you do that exemplifies each of Hillel's three questions?

The American Jewish Congress, in World War II's last year, promised to work "for a better world . . . whether or not the individual issues touch directly upon so-called Jewish interest." Jewish involvement was particularly significant in the Civil Rights, interfaith, antiwar, and feminist movements.

SHOULDER TO SHOULDER

For years, individual Jews had provided support, and even played leadership roles, in the National Association for the Advancement of Colored People (NAACP) and the National Urban League, both founded in the early twentieth century. Both the National Conference of Christians and Jews and the National Council of Churches supported racial equality after the war. Many Jews saw racism as a violation of their ethics, and realized that they had an interest in the affirmation of rights for all people. In 1947, the American Jewish Committee acknowledged the close relationship "between the protection of the civil rights of all citizens and the protection of the civil rights of the members of particular groups."

The Civil Rights movement found support across the American Jewish community. The Reform Central

Conference of American Rabbis celebrated Race Relations Day in 1953. Rabbi Leo Jung, an Orthodox rabbi in New York, praised the U.S. Supreme Court's 1954 *Brown v. Board of Education of Topeka, Kansas* decision. This decision outlawed racially segregated schools as a violation of the Fourteenth Amendment to the Constitution, declaring it a "red-letter day in American history."

Two rabbis who were Holocaust survivors—Rabbis Joachim Prinz and Abraham Joshua Heschel—took leading roles in the Civil Rights movement. Joachim Prinz was one of the organizers of the 1963 March on Washington. Some 250,000 people—black and white—gathered in the nation's capital to protest segregation and urge passage of the Civil Rights bill that President John F. Kennedy had sent to Congress. Prinz spoke at the rally, appearing just a few minutes before Dr. Martin Luther King, Jr., head of the Southern Christian Leadership Conference (SCLC) and the most prominent civil rights leader of the time, delivered his famous "I Have A Dream" speech. In his address, Prinz drew on his experience under the Nazis and called silence "the most shameful and the most tragic problem" in human responses to bigotry and persecution. A few years before, he had led a picket line in front of a Woolworth's, a discount store in New York City, protesting the company's policy of discrimination against African Americans at its lunch counters in stores across the South.

Think About It

Do you agree with Rabbi Prinz's opinion about silence? Why or why not?

Rabbi Abraham Joshua Heschel commented that, "racism is man's gravest threat to man—the maximum of hatred for a minimum of reason." He met King, who was known for preaching nonviolence, and the two became friends. At the National Conference on Religion and Race in January 1963, Heschel delivered his first major statement on civil rights, drawing connections between African Americans' struggle and the exodus of the Jews from Egypt. "In fact," Heschel said, "it was easier for the children of Israel to cross the Red Sea than for a Negro to cross certain university campuses." Called "Father Abraham" within the Civil Rights movement, Heschel took part in the 1965 march from Selma to Montgomery, Alabama. Describing that march, Heschel said, "I felt a sense of the Holy in what I was doing. . . . Even without words, our march was worship. I felt my legs were praying." [from Jonathan D. Sarna, *American Judaism: A History* (New Haven: Yale University Press, 2004)]

Think About It

What different forms can prayer take?

Many of the white college students who traveled to the South to support the movement during these years were Jews. In 1961, when white and black college students boarded buses throughout the South to challenge segregation on interstate buses and in

Do It

Write a poem, essay, song, or story, or create a work of art that communicates your emotions and thoughts about helping those in need outside the Jewish community.

Quoted by Martin Niemoller

Look At It

Martin Niemoller, a Protestant minister, made the following well-known statement, which reflects Hillel's words:

In Germany, the Nazis first came for the Communists, and I did not speak up because I was not a Communist. Then they came for the Jews, but I did not speak up because I was not a Jew. And then they came for the trade unionists, and I did not speak up because I was not a trade unionist. Then they came for the Catholics, but I was a Protestant, so I did not speak up. And then they came for me, and by that time there was no one left to speak up for anyone. To make sure this does not happen again, the injustice to anyone anywhere must be the concern of everyone everywhere.

[from Rabbi David A. Teutsch, ed., *Kol Haneshamah: Shabbat Vehagim* **(Wyncote, Pennsylvania: The Reconstructionist Press, 1994)]**

Abraham Joshua Heschel (second from right) marching with Dr. Martin Luther King, Jr. in Selma, Alabama

Southern bus stations, at least 30 percent of the white "freedom riders" were Jews. When the Student Non-Violent Coordinating Committee organized students to help blacks register to vote in Mississippi during what was called "Freedom Summer," in 1964, almost two-thirds of the white volunteers were Jews. Two of those Jewish activists—Andrew Goodman and Michael Schwerner—were murdered by members of the Ku Klux Klan.

A number of these Jewish volunteers were northern women who chose to join a movement to combat social injustice. Many had grown up as the children of immigrants in families that had struggled to become assimilated into the American mainstream. And while they may not have expressed strong religious identifications as Jews while in the movement, their Jewish backgrounds, traditions, politics, and values shaped their thinking and impelled their involvement. As one woman told her mother who was worried for her safety, "Mother, this is what you taught me to do, and this is what you taught me to be. If I don't do it, then I will not be true to all that you have taught me." [from Debra L. Schultz, "Going South: Jewish Women in the Civil Rights Movement," in Pamela S. Nadell, ed., *American Jewish Women's History: A Reader* (New York: New York University Press, 2003)]

By the mid 1960s, a number of strains appeared to be developing in the relationship between blacks and Jews. A new group of black leaders, including Malcolm X, Stokely Carmichael, and H. Rap Brown, and more recently Louis Farrakhan, emerged. They felt that empowerment—ownership and control of business and institutions serving the black community—was more important than Martin Luther King's dream of integration. Some of them engaged in outright antisemitism and viewed Israel negatively. Black-Jewish relations have become a source of much discussion between both groups in recent years.

Southern Jews, who were only a small minority in the region—barely 1 percent of the total population—had long been accepted by their neighbors. Most, therefore, were hesitant to question too openly the social customs of their hometowns. Beyond the major cities, where some Jews did dare to speak out and even to provide funds and other help to Civil Rights organizations, most Jews tended to remain quiet on the issue and quite a few were not pleased when Northern Jews traveled south to promote civil rights. In some Southern communities, if Jews hesitated to join White

It Shaped Their Thinking, Too

Many of the Jewish women civil rights activists were the children or grandchildren of Holocaust survivors, or grew up in a community of refugees. One, Gertrude Weissman Orris, joined her husband in Germany at the end of the war and, as she tells it, asked any German she met, "What did you do during the war?" One evening, a man answered her saying, "If you're asking me if I was a coward, I was a coward. I knew what was happening but I couldn't do anything about it. My best friend was taken away. Now let me ask you something—what are you going to do when your turn comes?" Orris was stunned and had difficulty answering at first. Then she replied that she did not know what she would do but hoped she would do the right thing. The man said, "What you hope and what you do are two different things."

Orris says that when she came back to the United States she "was a different person. I felt that the most important thing I could do is to work in the Black movement. If anything happened, then somebody didn't have to say to me, what did you do?" [from Debra L. Schultz, "Going South: Jewish Women in the Civil Rights Movement," in Pamela S. Nadell, ed., *American Jewish Women's History: A Reader* (New York: New York University Press, 2003)]

 Has any issue or movement ever affected you so strongly that you felt you simply had to take part in it? What was it and why? How did Judaism influence your decision?

Citizens Councils, there were consequences: money dried up at their banks, loans were called in, linen was not collected for cleaning at their restaurants, and the local police might harass store owners about "violations" of the fire code.

Most Southern congregations, therefore, requested that their rabbis maintain a low profile on the race issue. Generally the rabbis did so, although some took strong stands in favor of civil rights despite personal threats and the bombing of synagogues and other Jewish communal buildings, usually by the Klan. Despite this intimidation, about 50 percent of white civil rights lawyers in the South were Jews. They traveled throughout the region filing complaints on jailhouse beatings, requesting parade permits, and handling bail hearings.

There were some Jews who opposed the Civil Rights movement. In Mobile, Alabama, a significant number of Jews supported segregationist Governor George Wallace, who twice ran for president. Most Jews, however, supported the movement in its early years, and were, therefore, stunned and hurt when they realized that antisemitism was spreading among African Americans in the 1960s. The Black Muslim movement (also known as the Nation of Islam) led by Elijah Muhammad reached its peak during these years, and both antisemitism and anti-Israel sentiments were commonly expressed. Antisemitism was also part of the **rhetoric** of other black radical leaders.

 Rhetoric refers to the use of exaggeration in language.

 What might have caused this break between the Jewish and African American communities?

PROTESTANT-CATHOLIC-JEW

The 1955 book, *Protestant-Catholic-Jew*, by Will Herberg, analyzed these three religions and their impact on American culture. The book placed Jews, who made up only 3 percent of the population, on an equal footing with Christians in the United States. Herberg argued that Americans accepted all three faiths as components of the "American Way of Life." When American beliefs were described as Judeo-Christian, Jews saw this as yet additional evidence of their acceptance by non-Jews and an acknowledgment of Jews' contributions to the nation's development. These views led to the postwar interfaith movement dialogues between Jews and people of other religions.

Even before he became a part of the Civil Rights movement, Rabbi Heschel was active in the interfaith movement. When Pope John XXIII called for a gathering of cardinals and bishops at Vatican Council II, he included among its goals a new interpretation of Catholic teachings about Jews and Catholics' relationship with Jews. The American Jewish Committee asked Heschel to try to influence these deliberations, and he met in 1961 with a key German cardinal.

Heschel identified a few important issues that needed to be addressed and he urged Catholics "to reject and condemn those who assert that the Jews as a people are responsible for the crucifixion." In addition, he asked Catholics not to look at Jews only as potential converts but to "acknowledge the integrity and permanent preciousness of Jews and Judaism." Finally, he asked the Roman Catholic Church to reject antisemitism in the form of stereotypes or antisemitic actions. The final document approved by the Church fell short of Heschel's hopes, as it was not as specific as he had requested; however, it did improve relationships between Catholics and Jews.

Not all Jews, however, approved interfaith work. Rabbi Moshe Feinstein, president of the Orthodox Agudath HaRabonim, forbade Orthodox rabbis to take part in any interaction with Christian leaders because he believed these could lead to conversion. Rabbi Joseph Soloveitchik, speaking for the Rabbinical Council of America, was more open to communication, but said that interfaith connections "should occur not at a theological, but at a **mundane** human level."

 Mundane means "ordinary" or "routine."

 What is your opinion about the wisdom of interfaith dialogue? Why?

One major disappointment in the relationship between Christians and Jews came with the failure of some Christian institutions to be sufficiently sympathetic to Israel during the Six-Day War. The fact that both the National Conference of Catholic Bishops and the National Council of Churches did not endorse Israel

The Catholic Church's Nostra Aetate Declaration, October 28, 1965

Look At It

The Catholic Church issued a paper that declared:

Since Christians and Jews have such a common spiritual heritage, this sacred council wishes to encourage and further mutual understanding and appreciation. This can be obtained, especially, by way of biblical and theological enquiry and through friendly discussions.

Even though the Jewish authorities and those who followed their lead pressed for the death of Christ (John 19:6), neither all Jews indiscriminately at that time, nor Jews today, can be charged with the crimes committed during His passion. It is true that the church is the new people of God, yet the Jews should not be spoken of as rejected or accused . . .

Indeed, the Church reproves every form of persecution against whomsoever it may be directed. [from Jacob Rader Marcus, ed., *The Jew in the American World: A Source Book*, (Detroit, Michigan: Wayne State University Press, 1996.)]

Think About It — What is your reaction to this document?

JEWS AND THE VIETNAM WAR

After World War II, France gave up its claim to Vietnam, and the nation was divided into North and South Vietnam, with Communists in power in the North. When the leader of South Vietnam, Ngo Dinh Diem, seemed to be gaining strength, the Communist Viet Cong began trying to take over the South. President Eisenhower, and then President Kennedy, sent military advisers to help the government of South Vietnam.

Lyndon Johnson, who became president when Kennedy was assassinated, ordered an escalation of the war by bombing North Vietnam and sending more U.S. troops. The number of troops skyrocketed under Johnson's leadership from 16,000 in 1963 to 550,000 in 1968. He expected that this show of force would cause the Communists to surrender; in fact, the Communists decided to wait for the Americans to tire of the war and the uproar it was causing in the United States.

As the number of American troops in Vietnam grew, the antiwar movement grew with it. Rabbi Heschel played a leading role in this movement, helping to form the Clergy Concerned about Vietnam (later called Clergy and Laymen Concerned about Vietnam). His partners in this project, which began in 1965, were Richard J. Neuhaus, then a Protestant pastor, and Daniel Berrigan, a radical Catholic priest. Several Reform rabbis, including Maurice Eisendrath, were soon among the group's members. Dr. Martin Luther King, Jr. paid tribute to Heschel in a famous antiwar speech, "Beyond Vietnam."

counteracted much of the good will that had been built during the previous two decades. American Jews saw the possibility of another Holocaust. American Christians saw Israel as a strong country that had soundly defeated its Arab neighbors more than once. They did not understand the powerful link in the minds of most American Jews between Israel and the Holocaust. As Leonard Fein wrote, in 1988, "To be a Jew in America is to carry with you the consciousness of limitless savagery . . . not as an abstraction, but as a reality; not, God help us all, only as a memory, but also as a possibility." Later, when Christian groups called for U.S. policies less favorable to Israel, American Jews saw that, too, as a betrayal.

Do It — Much interfaith work involves learning about one another. Prepare a speech about Judaism to present to a church youth group. Focus on some core beliefs, some important rituals and what they represent, and certain key holidays and how they are celebrated.

The Synagogue Council of America, an umbrella group for the movements established in 1926, and other Jewish leaders endorsed the withdrawal of American troops from Vietnam in 1966. President Johnson was confused by Jewish opposition to the war, given that Jews did not oppose arms sales to Israel. Some Jewish organizations endorsed the war so that Johnson would continue to support Israel. The Union of Orthodox Jewish Congregations announced its support for the war in 1966, arguing that it was right for the United States to confront Communist **expansionism**.

The Clergy and Laymen Concerned about Vietnam took more radical action, including peaceful civil disobedience. In a "Statement on Conscience and **Conscription**," the group demanded a broader definition of conscientious objection to allow more young men to avoid being drafted into military service if they had ethical objections to the war. Heschel described his need to speak out in opposition to the war saying, "To speak about God and remain silent on Vietnam is **blasphemous**."

Expansionism is a policy of taking over territory that belongs to another country.

Conscription means being drafted, or compelled to serve, in the military.

Blasphemous means "not pious or reverent."

Do you see any conflict between American Jews' opposition to the Vietnam War and their desire to provide arms to Israel? Why or why not?

THE EARLY WOMEN'S MOVEMENT

The women's movement, in which Jewish women played major roles, emerged in the 1960s, laying the groundwork for a women's movement within Judaism that would reshape many synagogue practices. A major impetus for the movement was the writing of Betty Friedan, born Bettye Naomi Goldstein in 1921. Friedan surveyed her Smith College classmates on their opinions about their lives, and published her findings in her 1963 book,

The Feminine Mystique. She argued that women were victimized by widespread but subtle discrimination and harmed by values that placed them solely in the limited roles of wife and mother.

In 1966, Friedan became a cofounder of the National Organization for Women (NOW), an organization aimed at securing equal rights for women. Her cofounders—Susan Brownmiller, Shulamith Firestone, and Naomi Weinstein—were also Jewish. As president of NOW, Friedan campaigned to stop the practice of listing classified advertisements by gender and pushed for a larger role for women within government. She supported child-care centers for working mothers, legalizing abortion, and other changes that would free women to enter the work force in greater numbers. She resigned from NOW in 1970 and played a key role in planning the Women's Strike for Equality that same year, marking the fiftieth anniversary of the women's **suffrage** amendment.

Suffrage means the right to vote.

Another key figure in the early women's movement was Gloria Steinem, who was a cofounder of *New York* magazine in 1968 and *Ms.* magazine in 1971. Her grandmother, a Polish immigrant, had been president of the Ohio Women's Suffrage Association. Like Betty Friedan, Steinem was a Smith College graduate. She became a journalist after college. For a short period of time she worked as a *Playboy* Bunny as research for an article called "The Bunny's Tale" about the belittling of women by men. She was co-convener of the National Women's Political Caucus in 1971, and a year later helped create the Ms. Foundation for Women to help needy women and girls.

Even in the early 1960s, some Jewish women were already leading the kind of life these activists promoted. Thousands of Jewish women were lawyers, with about a dozen working as federal judges. Hundreds were working as doctors, and Rosalyn Yalow became the first American woman to receive the Nobel Prize for Medicine in 1977 for inventing a technique to measure the amount of insulin in the blood of adult diabetics. She refused a special women's award from the *Ladies' Home Journal* magazine because she felt she was being honored as a brilliant woman, not a brilliant scientist.

By asserting themselves in areas usually dominated by men, these Jewish women opened the door to challenging gender role practices in traditional Judaism.

Think About It — Some might argue that aspects of traditional Judaism restricted women in certain ways. How do you account for the fact that so many Jewish women succeeded in many "nontraditional" ways?

NOTHING SUCCEEDS LIKE SUCCESS

Jews in postwar America had succeeded in becoming an integral part of American life. Many, therefore, felt comfortable reaching out beyond their own people and country to support Jews in Israel and people of other faiths and races in the United States.

Quoting Betty Friedan

"The feminine **mystique** has succeeded in burying millions of American women alive."

"Men weren't really the enemy—they were fellow victims suffering from an outmoded masculine mystique that made them feel unnecessarily inadequate when there were no bears to kill."
[from http://womenshistory.about.com]

Learn It — **Mystique** is "a framework of ideas or beliefs constructed around a person or object."

Click On It — Click on this website http://womens history.about.com./library/qu/ for more about women's history.

Do It — Select one of the Jewish women discussed in this section and find out more about her life and accomplishments.

Do It — Interview a woman you know about the influence the women's movement had on her life.

Do It — Solve the Puzzle

Below is a quote from Abraham Joshua Heschel. Solve the puzzle of the mixed-up alphabet in order to read the quote.

A hint: 0=M, 8=I, Z=A, G=T, V=E

DSV1 8 DZH B3F1T 8 ZW089VW X2VEV9 5V352V

_____

13D GSZG 8 Z0 32W 8 ZW089V 481W 5V352V

_____

What is your opinion of Heschel's words?

_____

_____

_____

_____

UNIT 2 TIME LINE OF HISTORICAL EVENTS:
JEWS IN POSTWAR AMERICA AND BEYOND

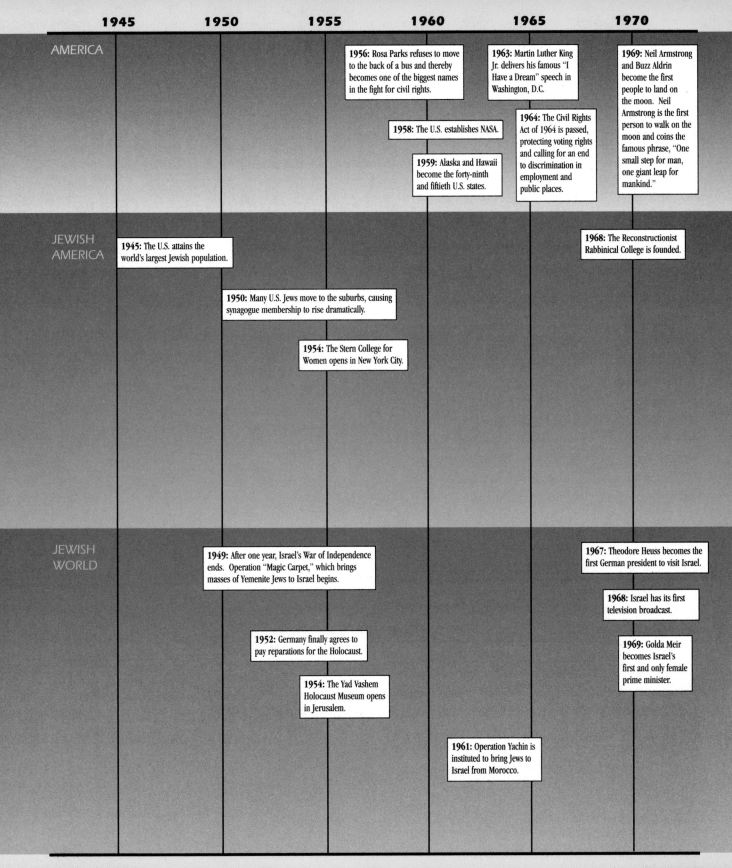

| 1945 | 1950 | 1955 | 1960 | 1965 | 1970 |

AMERICA

1956: Rosa Parks refuses to move to the back of a bus and thereby becomes one of the biggest names in the fight for civil rights.

1958: The U.S. establishes NASA.

1959: Alaska and Hawaii become the forty-ninth and fiftieth U.S. states.

1963: Martin Luther King Jr. delivers his famous "I Have a Dream" speech in Washington, D.C.

1964: The Civil Rights Act of 1964 is passed, protecting voting rights and calling for an end to discrimination in employment and public places.

1969: Neil Armstrong and Buzz Aldrin become the first people to land on the moon. Neil Armstrong is the first person to walk on the moon and coins the famous phrase, "One small step for man, one giant leap for mankind."

JEWISH AMERICA

1945: The U.S. attains the world's largest Jewish population.

1950: Many U.S. Jews move to the suburbs, causing synagogue membership to rise dramatically.

1954: The Stern College for Women opens in New York City.

1968: The Reconstructionist Rabbinical College is founded.

JEWISH WORLD

1949: After one year, Israel's War of Independence ends. Operation "Magic Carpet," which brings masses of Yemenite Jews to Israel begins.

1952: Germany finally agrees to pay reparations for the Holocaust.

1954: The Yad Vashem Holocaust Museum opens in Jerusalem.

1961: Operation Yachin is instituted to bring Jews to Israel from Morocco.

1967: Theodore Heuss becomes the first German president to visit Israel.

1968: Israel has its first television broadcast.

1969: Golda Meir becomes Israel's first and only female prime minister.

Reflect On It

How did American Jews help Jews around the world?
How did these campaigns shape the character of the American Jewish community?

American Jews, who had played a crucial role in the Civil Rights movement in the United States in the mid-1960s, began to look at the treatment of Jews in other countries as a human rights issue they could embrace. The Jewish communities of the Soviet Union and Ethiopia were suffering and crying out to their fellow Jews for help.

THE NEWS EMERGES

News of the Soviet Union's repression of the nation's nearly 2 million Jews began emerging in the late 1940s. Under Soviet leader Joseph Stalin, the Communists deported and imprisoned thousands of Jews and deprived them of their human rights. Israel set up a **covert** Liaison Bureau in 1952 to maintain contact with Soviet Jews and raise public awareness of their situation. The bureau's reports led to demonstrations against Soviet policy and top-level discussion of the issue between U.S. and Soviet officials.

At first, small steps were taken. Organizations were formed and protests began in 1964. Elie Wiesel published *The Jews of Silence* in 1966, after a trip to the Soviet Union. Following the 1967 Six-Day War, the issue moved to center stage as Russian Jews began opposing government regulations intended to prohibit Hebrew and Jewish education. A militant movement of people wishing to immigrate to Israel, their spiritual homeland, began to form.

 Learn It

Covert means "secret."

At first, the Soviet authorities thought that granting some of these Jews permission to emigrate would end the problem. However, news of a more liberal policy led thousands more to request such permission. They did so despite the fact that when the Soviet government decided to block further emigration, those who had applied faced demotions or the loss of their jobs. Jews who applied to leave and were refused by the Soviet Union were called "refuseniks." Once they were refused permission—usually with no explanation or the vague excuse of "state security"—and lost their jobs,

The Movement's Theme

During the early days of the movement to emigrate to Israel, one of the Russian Jewish protest songs was brought to the United States. The song repeats Moses's demand to Pharaoh (Exodus 7:16) saying, "Let my people go! Let the Jewish people go to its homeland."

Rabbi Shlomo Carlebach, a famous songwriter of the day, introduced *"Am Yisrael Chai,"* which became the movement's theme song. The words are *"Am Yisrael chai—Od avinu chai"* "The Jewish people live on—Still our fathers [the Patriarchs] live."

Think About It
Do you think the comparison of the Soviet Union to Egypt is an appropriate one? Why or why not?

it was impossible to find others because the government controlled employment. They could then be convicted of being "**parasites**" for not working and exiled to **Siberia**. The Soviet government sponsored trials, at which refuseniks were accused of anti-Soviet agitation and, often, treason. For most, their crime was nothing more than wanting to live in Israel. Jews who were imprisoned became known as "prisoners of conscience."

In 1970, the arrest and conviction for treason of Jews planning to hijack a plane from Leningrad to Israel drew more attention to the cause. Two received the death penalty and eleven were sent to prison for sentences ranging from fifteen years to life. The death sentences were eventually commuted due to an international and highly publicized protest. Soviet Jews sent thousands of letters and petitions to their own government and influential people in the West, informing them of their plight and calling for help.

A **parasite** is someone who or something that lives off of another without giving anything useful in return.

Siberia is a territory in eastern Russia to which many Soviet prisoners were sent.

THE SITUATION HEATS UP

The struggle for Soviet Jewry came to be seen as a Jewish civil rights struggle—a new priority for American Jews. The more intense focus on the problems of other Jews showed American Jews how much they could accomplish. Feeling that existing Jewish communal organizations were not doing enough, activists founded independent **grassroots** groups in the United States. Their goal was pressuring Soviet officials to allow Jews to emigrate. The activist groups disagreed with established organizations over tactics (quiet diplomacy versus noisy demonstrations) and policy (the necessity of Soviet émigrés going to Israel versus any other country they chose).

A **grassroots** movement is organized and directed by average people who are not usually considered politically influential.

Prepare to debate either of these issues: quiet diplomacy versus noisy demonstrations or the necessity of Soviet Jews making aliyah versus free choice of destination. Decide which of these two issues you will debate and which side you will take. List several arguments in support of your opinion.

An Activist Remembers

Connie and Joseph Smuckler, of Philadelphia, were among the first to become involved with Russian Jews, and they helped push the movement to the front of the Jewish community's agenda. Many activists went to Russia personally, visiting with refuseniks and smuggling in prayerbooks and other ritual items. Connie Smuckler recalled her visits saying:

Soviet Jewry protest march near Philadelphia's City Hall

"The Soviet Jews were joyous, because they knew . . . that we were going to tell their story. . . . it wasn't even so much what we brought them . . . the items were good because we collected and we got people involved . . . but it was much more. . . . They said, 'You are keeping us alive because somebody in the West knows that we're here,' and that's what they said made it different, between their movement and what happened in the Holocaust, because [then] nobody knew. . . . we tried to put a face and a name to every refusenik, and it just made the difference . . . people here wanted to go and meet them, because they were like us."

The Dream

Pamela Cohen, former national president of the Union of Councils for Soviet Jews, one of the grassroots organizations, stated about the movement:

Look At It

"Our dream was inviolate and unshakable. We were defiant and unrelenting and stubborn, and we fought on every front: We fought when Jews were fired from their jobs after they applied to emigrate, and we fought when they were stripped of academic degrees in public humiliation. We fought when they were denied medical attention, and fought for the right of our people in the prisons and labor camps. We fought anti-Semitic article by anti-Semitic article and we knew that every battle . . . had to be won. . . . We knew that our momentum and determination would eventually crescendo into a force that would ultimately rip open the gates."

[from Micah H. Naftalin, "The Activist Movement" in *A Second Exodus: The American Movement to Free Soviet Jews*, Murray Friedman and Albert Chernin, eds. (Hanover: University of New England Press, 1999)]

In 1971, the National Conference on Soviet Jewry, working with other mainstream Jewish groups, organized a World Conference on Soviet Jewry in Brussels. David Ben-Gurion joined 765 delegates who attended lectures and rallies holding signs with slogans such as "Save Soviet Jewry" and "Let My People Go." At the same time, Jews throughout the United States held candlelight vigils outside Soviet consulates and business offices and Jewish leaders designated "Remembrance Days" and "Sabbaths of Concern." Many people wore bracelets with refuseniks' names. The Student Struggle for Soviet Jewry (SSSJ), an organization of high school and college-age students founded in 1964, was one of the groups that had a significant impact.

As worldwide interest grew, more Soviet Jews—including the best educated and most accepted in Soviet society—faced increasing discrimination and applied for exit visas. The Soviet Union began easing emigration for

Do It — Ask your relatives, rabbis, or teachers whether they attended rallies or vigils for Soviet Jewry and to describe the experience.

Do It — Create a poster to use at a Soviet Jewry rally.

some people, while others faced new barriers, including a "diploma" tax, a fee intended to reimburse the government for education costs. The price of an exit visa rose in direct relation to the level of education each potential émigré had received. For a graduate of a technical institute, a visa was only $7,700; for a medical doctor it was $18,400; and for someone with a Ph.D. in a scientific field it was $20,000.

Congress passed the Jackson-Vanik amendment, named after its congressional sponsors, that pressured Soviets to improve their treatment of Jews and allow more emigration.

The Soviet government dropped the "diploma tax" and increased the total number of exit visas to 35,000 over the course of a year.

Think About It — Do you believe the United States has the right or the responsibility to attempt to change other nations' policies when they are discriminatory and unfair? How does your Judaism influence your opinion on this issue? Consider this quote from the Babylonian Talmud (*Shabbat* 54b): "Whoever can stop . . . the people of his city from sinning, but does not . . . is held responsible for the sins of the people of his city. If he can stop the whole world from sinning, and does not, he is held responsible for the sins of the whole world."

A CONTINUING CAMPAIGN

Jews around the country continued to protest, drawing attention to the plight of Soviet Jews. Jewish schools and synagogues "adopted" refusenik families or "prisoners of conscience," and many students who were becoming *b'nei mitzvah* paired with a Russian "twin," a Jewish student in the Soviet Union who was not permitted to have the ceremony. Following conferences in Brussels and Philadelphia in 1976, leaders of non-Jewish religious communities joined in demanding that the Soviet Union end its persecution of Jews. On "Solidarity Sunday" more than 150,000 people participated in the biggest march of the year, culminating in a huge rally at the United Nations in New York City.

People throughout the world were especially touched by the plight of Anatoly (Natan) Sharansky who was arrested in 1977 and accused of treason. At his trial, where he could have been sentenced to death, he made a speech that became known to Jews throughout the world and was often read at Passover seders. Although President Jimmy Carter publicly denied the charge that Sharansky had worked for the Central Intelligence Agency, Sharansky was sentenced to thirteen years in prison.

While many Russian Jews moved to Israel some came to the U.S. Many of these immigrants were doctors, lawyers, engineers, and artists, but because their English was often poor and the United States' licensing requirements for certain jobs were different from those in the Soviet Union, they had to accept lower-status work.

Click On It

You can read autobiographies of activists for Soviet Jewry online in an exhibit called "Women Who Dared" by the Jewish Women's Archive. Go to www.jwa.org/exhibits/wwd. One of the women is Galina Nizhnikov Veremkroit and another is Roz Garber.

About 250,000 Jews had left the Soviet Union by 1985, and almost 105,000 had settled in the United States. When Soviet leader Mikhail Gorbachev visited President Reagan in Washington, D.C. in 1987, 250,000 people gathered on the National Mall for "Freedom Sunday," the Soviet Jewry advocacy movement's largest rally. In 1989 and 1990, Gorbachev allowed another large group of Jews to leave, and American Jewish leaders

Sharansky's Speech

Sharansky's case was the subject of cover stories in both *Time* and *Newsweek* magazines. He refused to confess and made the following speech before the Soviet court:

"Five years ago I submitted my application for exit to Israel. Now I am further than ever from my dream. It would seem to be cause for regret. But . . . I am happy that I lived honestly, in peace with my conscience. I never compromised my soul, even under the threat of death. . . . For more than 2,000 years the Jewish people, my people, have been dispersed. But wherever they are, wherever Jews are found, each year they have repeated, 'Next year in Jerusalem.' Now . . . I say, turning to my people. . . . Next year in Jerusalem! And I turn to you, the court, who were required to confirm a predetermined sentence: to you I have nothing to say."

Look At It

Natan Sharansky was released from prison in February 1986 and moved to Israel where he became actively involved in national politics. He has published his memoir, *Fear No Evil*.

Do It

Look in a Haggadah to see if it includes Sharansky's speech or other prayers for Soviet Jews. Does your family recite them? Do you include other prayers or readings for other Jews who are oppressed?

Natan Sharansky

Poster and button from the Soviet Jewry advocacy movement

launched "Operation Passage to Freedom," a plan to relocate Soviet Jews to the United States rather than Israel. Israeli officials and many American Jewish advocates were outraged. And, with Gorbachev ending the persecution that had given Soviet Jews status as refugees, the American government backed away from a large role in accepting and funding the resettlement of Soviet Jews. Thus, in 1990, the American Jewish community launched "Operation Exodus," with the specific goal of redirecting Soviet Jews to Israel.

A total of over 1.5 million Soviet Jews left for Israel, the U.S., and Western Europe. With the collapse of the Soviet Union in 1991, the Jews still living in the countries that had formed the Soviet Union had to evaluate their attitude toward Judaism and their desire to remain in their homelands. The American Jewish community that had seen how much American Jews could do to help their fellow Jews, remained committed to helping them.

Over 2,00 years ago King Solomon and the Queen of Sheba moved to Ethiopia. Their descendants called themselves *Beta Yisrael*, "House of Israel," while non-Jewish Ethiopians called them "*Falashas*" (strangers). In the late 1970s, facing poverty, famine, and a brutal government that allowed no one to leave, Ethiopian Jews escaped to Sudan where conditions were not much better.

Israel and some private organizations began trying to rescue these Jews and move them to Israel in 1979. This was accomplished by using a secret airstrip in the desert near the refugee camps. By 1984, most of the Jews then in the camps had been rescued, but as this news reached Ethiopian villages, the small number of Jewish refugees turned into a flood.

Realizing that it could not handle this crisis alone, Israel asked the United States for help. Sudan was suffering from political unrest and an unstable government, and when the Sudanese envoy also requested American assistance in 1984, the State Department argued that allowing the United States to help evacuate the Ethiopian Jews was in Sudan's best economic interest. An evacuation, later named Operation Moses, took place between November 21, 1984, and January 5, 1985. Every night, except on Shabbat, a planeload of Jews was flown from the camps to Khartoum, the capital of Sudan, and then on to Brussels, Belgium, before finally arriving in Israel. In all, about 7,800 Ethiopian Jews came to Israel during Operation Moses.

When the news media discovered its secret deal to help relocate the Jewish refugees, Sudan ended the campaign. About 2,000 refugees were believed to remain in the camps. The U.S. government helped arrange another evacuation with the conditions that it be handled quickly, in a single maneuver by the United States, and that the flights not go directly to Israel.

Jews in Ethiopia

Operation Sheba relied on Ethiopian Jews who had already escaped to Israel to identify the remaining Jews in the camps. Camouflaged U.S. transports flew into an airstrip about eight miles from the camps. Instead of the expected 2,000 refugees, they found only 494 refugees and three of the four planes left Sudan with no passengers. Despite these latest secret arrangements, U.S. pilots flew directly to Eilat, Israel, where the refugees met Prime Minister Shimon Peres.

Later reports indicated that some Jews were left in the camps and that thousands remained in Ethiopia. In 1991, Operation Solomon was launched by Israel's foreign intelligence service, Mossad, after Ethiopia's tyrannical leader, Mengistu Haile Mariam, fled the country. The Jews, who had walked from their villages in remote areas of the country to Addis Ababa, the capital of Ethiopia, were packed onto planes and almost 20,000 flew to Israel. Some two-thirds of the refugees were children, including ten who were born during the airlift.

Before, during, and after these formal operations, representatives of American volunteer organizations visited Ethiopia and brought Jews out in other ways; for example, providing them with scholarships to western universities. The United Jewish Appeal–Federation of New York conducted a special mission to Ethiopia in 2003 to check on the condition of the Jews who remained there. They lived in poverty and had become partly assimilated into the Christian culture, which slowed the process of removing them from Ethiopia. Only about 250 a month were being processed for resettlement in Israel.

Many African Americans were impressed by American Jews' commitment to aid their African fellow Jews. As American Jews involved themselves in the rescue of Jews in other lands, their deeds were positive testimony to the Jewish belief that we are our brothers' keepers.

To learn more about the rescue of Ethiopian Jews, go to www. nacoej.org, the website of the North American Conference on Ethiopian Jewry.

Newly arrived Ethiopian Jews learn Hebrew in Israel.

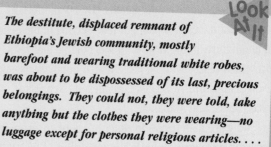

Do It

"Am I my brother's keeper?" is the question Cain asks God (Genesis 4:9) in response to God's inquiry about Abel. Rabbi Joseph Telushkin has said that the entire Torah is a positive response to this question. What do you think? List things that you do to be your "brother's keeper."

A Journey to Freedom

Read the following account of Operation Solomon by Helen Davis:

Look At It

The destitute, displaced remnant of Ethiopia's Jewish community, mostly barefoot and wearing traditional white robes, was about to be dispossessed of its last, precious belongings. They could not, they were told, take anything but the clothes they were wearing—no luggage except for personal religious articles....

For most, it was not only a journey from Ethiopia to Israel, from peril to safety, from exile to home, but also a journey from the seventeenth century to the twentieth century . . . their first encounter with the modern world....

[from Jacob Rader Marcus, ed., *The Jew in the American World: A Source Book* (Detroit: Wayne State University Press, 1996)]

CHAPTER 8

STRENGTHENING THE COMMUNITY

In what ways did Jews contribute to American life as a whole? In what ways did they strengthen their own Jewish community?

By the latter half of the twentieth century, Jews had become part of mainstream America. As prejudice decreased, they could focus their energies on promoting the general welfare of all Americans, as well as building the American Jewish community. Some of them tried to blend into the larger society. Others, however, were clearly affected by their Jewish upbringing and acknowledged that influence openly.

JEWS INFLUENCE AMERICAN POLITICAL LIFE

The years between 1950 and 2000 saw a dramatic rise in the number of Jewish politicians. In 1952 there was only one Jewish senator, representing New York, and there were only a few Jews in the House of Representatives, all from cities with large Jewish populations. By 1980, this had changed dramatically, with eight Jews serving in the Senate and about thirty in the House. It was notable that Jews represented places without large Jewish populations, such as New Hampshire, Wisconsin, Minnesota, Nebraska, Kansas, Texas, and Alabama.

Jews were also found in other areas of government in increasing numbers. John F. Kennedy, elected in 1960, had two Jews in his Cabinet—Arthur Goldberg and Abraham Ribicoff. In the 1970s, Richard Nixon made Henry Kissinger the nation's first Jewish secretary of state. New York City had its first two Jewish mayors during this time. Abraham Beame was elected in 1973 and served two terms before losing to Edward Koch, who stressed his Jewishness to boost his electability in a city where over 10% of the population was Jewish. Koch helped New York City avoid bankruptcy.

 Do you think it is important for Jews to be involved in American politics? Why or why not?

One of the first Jewish women to make a strong mark on Washington, D.C. was Bella Abzug. In 1970, at the age of fifty, Abzug was the first woman elected to Congress on a women's rights and peace platform. She coauthored such significant legislation as the Freedom of Information Act, making it easier for ordinary Americans to get access to previously secret government documents, and helped create the congressional caucus on women's issues and the National Women's Political Caucus. A Zionist since the age of ten, Abzug actively supported Israel in Congress. After leaving the House, she led the fight against the "Zionism is Racism" resolution in the United Nations, insisting that Zionism was a liberation movement.

Other Jewish women

Bella Abzug

also held powerful positions in office. Dianne Feinstein served as mayor of San Francisco before becoming a U.S. Senator in 1993. That same year, Ruth Bader Ginsburg became the first Jewish woman to serve on the U.S. Supreme Court. She became a lawyer and was the second woman to teach on the faculty of Rutgers Law School, and tried many cases for the American Civil Liberties Union before the Supreme Court. President Jimmy Carter appointed her to the U.S. Court of Appeals for the District of Columbia. When President Bill Clinton had a vacancy to fill on the Supreme Court, he nominated her.

In 2000, Senator Joseph Lieberman of Connecticut, an Orthodox Jew, was the Democratic nominee for vice president of the United States on a ticket led by then-vice president Al Gore. Although the Gore-Lieberman ticket won the popular vote, the Republican ticket of George W. Bush and Dick Cheney won a majority of votes in the Electoral College and took the election. A member of two Orthodox synagogues, one in Connecticut and one in Washington, D.C., Lieberman would not campaign on Shabbat. He would, however, attend important meetings and votes in Congress, walking several miles to get there, when necessary. A strong supporter of Israel, he cosponsored the Jerusalem Embassy Act of 1995 that asked the president to move the American embassy from Tel Aviv to Jerusalem but the embassy remained in Tel Aviv.

Click On It

To read other famous American Jews' statements about being Jewish, click on www.ajc.org/JewishLife/BeingJewishDetail

What Being Jewish Means to Me

from "What Being Jewish Means to Me," The American Jewish Committee, www.ajc.org/JewishLife

Look At It

Justice Ruth Bader Ginsburg is very proud of her Judaism. In an address to the annual meeting of the American Jewish Committee (May, 1995) she stated:

I am a judge born, raised, and proud of being a Jew. The demand for justice runs through the entirety of the Jewish tradition. I hope, in my years on the bench of the Supreme Court of the United States, I will have the strength and courage to remain constant in the service of that demand.

Senator Lieberman made a statement about being Jewish that appeared in *The New York Times* on December 6, 1992, in which he said:

To me, being Jewish means having help in answering life's most fundamental questions, such as, "How did I come to this place?" and, "Now that I am here, how should I live?"

. . . Being Jewish in America also means feeling a special love for this country. . . . My parents raised me to believe that I did not have to mute my religious faith or ethnic identity to be a good American, that, on the contrary, America invites all its people to be what they are and believe what they wish.

Do It

Write your answer to the question: What does being Jewish mean to me? Then, interview people in your community and ask them the same question.

JEWS IN THE ARTS AND SCIENCES

Jews have influenced American cultural life almost since their arrival in the country. Since World War II, their prominence in the sciences has been unmistakable and has benefited Jews and non-Jews alike. European Jewish physicists, chemists, and mathematicians came to the United States both before and after the war and contributed to the development of the atomic bomb, genetic analysis, and advancements in mathematics. Jews also enriched the study of art history, economics, sociology, and political science.

Although right after the war some quotas still kept Jews out of academia, by the 1950s the barriers were falling. Jews took their places on the faculties of graduate schools and research institutions, and by the 1970s they could be found among the deans of law schools within the prestigious Ivy League. By 1987, when a Jew was confirmed as president of Princeton University, Jews had already served as presidents of Dartmouth, Columbia, and the University of Pennsylvania.

Law and medicine were popular career choices among Jews, and the American Bar Association chose its first Jewish president in 1966. By the late 1960s, most big-city law firms had at least one Jewish senior partner. Jews' desires to practice medicine, even during the time of quotas, helped spread Jewish hospitals throughout the country. By the 1970s, these hospitals were serving mostly non-Jewish patients. As the number of Jewish doctors rose, they played an exceptionally large role in the field of psychology. When the 1988 edition of *Who's Who in America* came out, Jews represented one in five doctors listed when they made up under 4% of the population of the country.

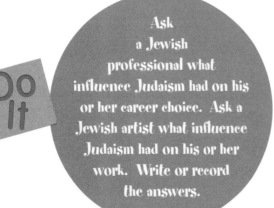

Ask a Jewish professional what influence Judaism had on his or her career choice. Ask a Jewish artist what influence Judaism had on his or her work. Write or record the answers.

Jews also played a big role in the arts. Actor Marlon Brando once told an interviewer that, "Jews have contributed more to American . . . culture than any other single group." Without them "we wouldn't have music," "we wouldn't have much theater," and we wouldn't have "all the songs that you love to sing."

While some American Jewish artists hesitated to make their work "too Jewish" in an effort to be acceptable to a wide audience, by the late twentieth century others had begun to explore their Jewish culture openly and proudly. The National Foundation for Jewish Culture stated: "We are in the midst of a Jewish cultural renaissance in America. When you see feature films reflecting the Jewish experience in your local Cineplex, attend readings of new Jewish writing in your local bookstore, listen to new Jewish music in downtown jazz clubs, visit thousands of Jewish websites on the Internet, take courses in Jewish Studies on college campuses across the country—there can be little doubt that we are in a Golden Age of Jewish Culture unlike any in the four-thousand-year history of the Jewish people." [from Jonathan Sarna, *American Judaism: A History* (New Haven: Yale University Press, 2004)]

 Think About It Do you think that it is important that Jewish writers, artists, and musicians make their work recognizably Jewish? Why or why not?

Music—both classical and popular—was a realm in which Jews shone. Longtime opera star, Beverly Sills, became general director of the New York City Opera Company. Conductor and composer Leonard Bernstein is known for such popular works as the score for *West Side Story*, as well as symphonic works with Jewish themes.

Other Jewish composers, such as Oscar Hammerstein II and Richard Rodgers, Frederick Loewe and Alan Jay Lerner, and Stephen Sondheim were known for their work on Broadway. Some Broadway shows, which were later turned into movies, involved Jewish themes as well as Jewish stars. Barbra Streisand played comic and singer Fannie Brice in the autobiographical *Funny Girl*, and Zero Mostel was Tevye in *Fiddler on the Roof*, a nostalgic look at life in the Eastern European *shtetlech*, based on the work of Sholem Aleichem. Other films confronted Jewishness directly such as *The Pawnbroker* and *Bye Bye Braverman* in the 1960s, *Hester Street* in the 1970s, and *Crossing Delancey* in the 1980s.

Watch one of the movies named in the text and write a review. Does it portray a positive view of Jews and Judaism? Do you relate to the characters as Jews? How do you feel about Jewish issues being treated in a popular forum such as a movie?

Richard Rogers and Oscar Hammerstein II

Playwrights and writers such as Arthur Miller, Chaim Potok, Saul Bellow, Bernard Malamud, Philip Roth, Rebecca Goldstein, and Allegra Goodman explored Jewish issues, such as the Jew's connection to religion, culture, tradition, and history, in popular American fiction. Jewish book, film, and folk festivals that one rabbi described as "a uniquely American way to celebrate Judaism" became popular. Jewish museums—more than fifty in twenty-two states—dedicated to preserving, exploring, and celebrating Jewish culture were built. Jews wanted to know about Jewishness and Jewish identity, and wealthy Jewish collectors were willing to purchase major works and donate them to help create these institutions.

Some of these works, and the museums that housed them, were dedicated to the memory of the Holocaust. The 1978 television miniseries, *Holocaust*; the establishment of the President's Commission on the Holocaust that same year; the annual Holocaust commemoration in the Capitol Rotunda beginning in 1979; the introduction of Holocaust curricula in public schools in the mid 1970s; the opening of the United States Holocaust Memorial Museum in 1993; and the release of Steven Spielberg's film, *Schindler's List*, later that year all heightened public awareness of those tragic days.

To learn more about the U.S. Holocaust Memorial Museum click on www.ushm.org.

MOVING AWAY FROM THE MAINSTREAM

In the late 1960s some American Jews wanted to express both pride in their religious heritage and their negative feelings about "the establishment," mainstream Jewish organizations. Fearing that American Judaism would not survive unless it changed, they developed new initiatives so that their Judaism would take on new life and meaning. They wanted to blend Judaism with their secular lives as well as the **counterculture** ideas of the time.

Counterculture is the way of life of those people who reject the established values and behavior of society.

Mordecai Kaplan had outlined his "Program for the Reconstruction of Judaism" in 1920 and published the book that expounded on his philosophy, *Judaism as a Civilization*, in 1934. Although he expressed no desire to establish an alternative Jewish "movement," in the 1950s he allowed the formation of a few Reconstructionist clubs. The Reconstructionist Fellowship of Congregations (now known as the Jewish Reconstructionist Federation) was founded in 1955, but there were only ten member groups by 1968. That year, Kaplan approved the formation of the Reconstructionist Rabbinical College in Philadelphia, which marked the emergence of Reconstructionism as a separate movement in American Judaism. Rabbi Ira Eisenstein, Kaplan's son-in-law and a major leader of the new movement, became the RRC's first president. Also in 1968, the Reconstructionist movement recognized as Jewish the child of a Jewish father and non-Jewish mother, as long as the child was raised as a Jew. **Patrilineal** descent, a radical change in the definition of who is a Jew, was adopted by the Reform movement as well in 1983. Thus, Reconstructionism, while the smallest of the four American Jewish religious movements, was at the forefront of measures to adapt Judaism to the values of liberal America.

Patrilineal means tracing one's identity through the father's ancestry. In defining Jews, only matrilineal descent had been previously considered.

You can learn more about the Reconstructionist Rabbinical College by clicking on www.rrc.edu.

A push for more radical political change took place on college campuses during the 1960s. The "Jewish Left," which emerged after 1967, supported the emigration of Soviet Jews; campaigned for university Jewish Studies programs; criticized the Jewish "establishment"; and wanted Jews to pay greater attention to Judaism's emphasis on *tzedakah* and helping people. The Jewish Left explained its ideas in new magazines such as *Response*.

During this time, the Jewish "counterculture" scorned established Jewish organizations and began to embrace a movement that, in some ways, resembled the secular **communes** of the period. Young activists felt that the community's values were misguided and could find nothing worthwhile in synagogues that elevated "success, wealth, and **rote** religious performance," as they put it, above everything else. They saw the family in an equally negative light, and called for "real community" and "real intimacy."

In 1968, the ancient rabbinic term *havurah* was used to identify a group that became one of the most exciting—and enduring—of the new initiatives. Havurat Shalom was founded in Somerville, Massachusetts, as a seminary. It soon developed into an experimental community in which members explored new forms of ritual

and, ultimately, decided not to have a rabbi. Soon after, the New York Havurah, Farbrangen in Washington, and a *havurah* in Philadelphia were founded. Members were interested in such issues as social justice and Jewish diversity, and in involving everyone in Jewish learning. Services were often informal. Congregations led prayers and conducted discussions in place of sermons. As one *havurah* founder put it, members "wanted to create a participant community rather than to be in a large impersonal institution in which culture or religion was dished out to us. We didn't want to be an audience, we wanted to be the *kahal* [community]."

Communes are relatively small communities, often rural. The residents of a commune share labor, interests, and wealth. Usually, property is owned by the entire group rather than one individual. Many such communes were established during the 1960s.

Rote means repetitive without thinking about something's meaning.

Havurah comes from the Hebrew term *haver* which means "friend" or "companion." It is a group that learns and prays together.

What aspects of your synagogue help you to feel part of a community?

The *havurah* movement spread during the 1970s with the organization of groups on many college campuses. These *havurot* had a democratic structure and often sponsored communal study, shared meals, and retreats. Members of the Jewish Left saw them as an alternative to the Judaism of suburban America, allowing for more intimate fellowship within the community and greater spiritual growth than could be had in large synagogues.

Traditional Jewish institutions could not ignore the *havurot*. As Conservative Rabbi Stephen Lerner wrote in 1970, "If the *havurah* does nothing else, it should remind Jewish leaders that . . . religious creativity, **fervor**, and a sense of community have not passed from this earth." *The Jewish Catalog*, written by members of Havurat Shalom and published in 1973 by the Jewish Publication Society, was designed to help readers "live and experience Jewish life in a creative and personal way." Its popularity showed that the do-it-yourself message of the *ḥavurot* held great attraction for many American Jews. Over the next decades, many synagogues adopted some practices of the *ḥavurot*, or formed *ḥavurot* within them, and many *ḥavurah* members eventually rejoined synagogues. Thus, the *ḥavurah* movement's emphasis on spirituality and **renewal** changed the way Judaism was practiced across the spectrum of Jewish life.

 Learn It

Fervor means "passion."

Renewal is a rebirth, the process of making something old seem new and exciting again.

Some Reform Jews now returned to once discarded rituals and practices—such as wearing *kippot* and *tallitot*. The Conservative movement issued a statement of principles that recognized "variations of practice" while calling on Conservative Jews "to maintain the laws and practices of the past as much as possible." Members of both movements updated and reinterpreted rituals to make them more personally meaningful.

The Orthodox movement added thousands of new young members at this time who, while not born Orthodox, became *ba'ale teshuva* [returning Jews] hoping to find meaning in the rituals of traditional Judaism. At the same time, many Jews born and raised Orthodox were showing increased and outward signs of their Jewish identity, such as wearing *kippot* in public.

The renewal of spiritual practices was also fueled by a few charismatic leaders—most of whom were originally connected with the Lubavitch movement—who focused on music, meditation, and prayer, and attracted followers from all walks of Jewish life. Rabbi Shlomo Carlebach, who was known as "The Dancing Rabbi," "The Singing Rabbi," and sometimes "The Hippie Rabbi," touched thousands of people through his Jewish folk music.

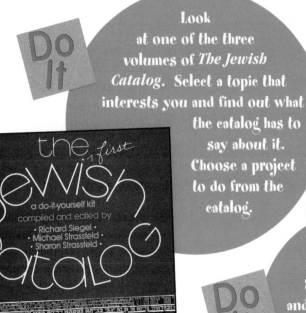

Do It
Look at one of the three volumes of *The Jewish Catalog*. Select a topic that interests you and find out what the catalog has to say about it. Choose a project to do from the catalog.

The cover of *The First Jewish Catalog*

Do It
Listen to the music of Shlomo Carlebach and/or Debbie Friedman. Pick a song that moves you to learn and teach to your class.

Girls performing at Hillel in the early 1970s

Rabbi Zalman Schachter-Shalomi, known as Reb Zalman, founded the Jewish Spiritual Renewal movement, which emphasized building community, enhancing spirituality, encouraging participation, and promoting gender equality. An Orthodox woman, *Rebbetzin* Esther Jungreis, the wife of a rabbi, inspired a movement called "*Hineni*" [here I am], dedicated to winning young Jews back to traditional Judaism. Singer-songwriter Debbie Friedman, who offers mainstream Jews "a sense of spiritual connectedness," performs in packed concert halls, and has recorded more than a dozen albums. Her music is part of the liturgy in many congregations. [from Jonathan D. Sarna, *American Judaism: A History* (New Haven: Yale University Press, 2004)]

American Jews' interest in Jewish education grew. Pre-schools, day schools, supplementary schools, university Jewish studies programs, and adult schools all benefited from the this growth. Greater numbers of Jews in America received more Jewish education than ever before.

JEWISH WOMEN HAVE A DRAMATIC EFFECT

Jewish women had been playing prominent roles in the national feminist movement and some now turned their attention to what they saw as unfair practices within Judaism. Equality for women was not a new issue for American Judaism, but it now took on new importance as a symbol of the conflict between tradition and modern life in America. In 1971, a group of largely Conservative women formed *Ezrat Nashim* [meaning "assistance of women," the phrase also refers to the women's section in the synagogue], seeking "an end to the second-class status of women in Jewish life." A year later, the group's members were uninvited guests at the annual Rabbinical Assembly meeting of Conservative rabbis, and they arrived with a list of demands. Their goals included allowing women to be counted in a minyan and to participate fully in religious observances; serve as witnesses under Jewish law; initiate Jewish divorce proceedings; attend rabbinical and cantorial schools and perform rabbinical and cantorial functions; play a role in synagogues; and

Gloria Steinem

Do It

Do research about any of the issues mentioned to find out why women were not traditionally permitted to participate in these ways.

fulfill all mitzvot just as men did.

About 400 women participated in the National Jewish Women's Conference in 1973, and during the next year women continued to meet in small groups around the country. At a second national meeting in 1974, a group called the Jewish Feminist Organization established regional offices around the United States and in Canada. The organization's goals stated, "We, Jewish feminists, have joined together here in strength and joy to struggle for the liberation of the Jewish woman." It developed a speakers' bureau, conducted workshops, and helped those trying to make changes within their own synagogues. In 1976, Jewish feminists published *Lilith*, a magazine that sought to expand women's roles inside the synagogue as well as within the Jewish community.

Click On It

You can learn more about *Lilith* magazine by clicking on www.lilith.org.

A key concern for Jewish women was the fact that none of the movements had yet ordained a woman rabbi. The Reform sisterhood organization raised the issue in the early 1960s, as young women began to play more active leadership roles in youth activities. Some even attended classes at the Hebrew Union College, and in 1968, Sally Priesand moved into the rabbinical track at the Hebrew Union College–Jewish Institute of Religion in Cincinnati. She was ordained in 1972; two years later, Sandy Eisenberg Sasso became the first Reconstructionist woman rabbi. By the end of the twentieth century, women made up at least half of rabbinical students within both the Reform and Reconstructionist movements. The Reform movement had ordained 335 women by 2000, while the smaller Reconstructionist movement had ordained ninety-eight.

The Conservative movement debated the ordination of women from 1972 to 1983. Women were playing broader roles in many Conservative synagogues. After 1973, many counted women as part of the minyan, and by 1983, most did so. More than three-quarters of Conservative synagogues called women up to the Torah by 1983. In October of that year, the faculty voted to allow women into the rabbinical school of the Jewish Theological Seminary. Amy Eilberg became the first Conservative woman rabbi in 1985, and 150 additional women had been ordained by 2000.

In the Reform, Conservative, and Reconstructionist movements, women now led services, read Torah, and were sensitive to language issues such as prayers that addressed God as male or excluded the **matriarchs**. Synagogues introduced gender-sensitive prayer books; traditional life-cycle ceremonies, such as marriage,

became **egalitarian**; and new rituals, such as the baby-naming ceremony for girls (*simḥat bat*) were created.

Matriarchs are mothers. In Judaism this refers to Sarah, Rebekah, Rachel, and Leah.

Egalitarian is the belief in the equality of all people.

Although Orthodox Judaism remained firmly opposed to many of these changes, especially the ordination of women, it, too, was touched by the feminist movement. High level Jewish education for girls and women became more common as did bat mitzvah ceremonies. Modern Orthodox leaders permitted women to form their own prayer groups to study the Talmud. In Brooklyn, women founded "Getting Equal Treatment" (GET), a group dedicated to requiring husbands to grant religious divorces to their wives. A religious divorce is a *get*; without one, a woman cannot remarry. Many synagogues found themselves divided on issues such as whether women could read from the Torah scroll in female-only groups. Clearly, much had changed in Jewish life in America in response to the new challenges presented by living in America.

Do It — Word Search

Find the names or terms from Unit 3 listed below. Look up, down, diagonally, left, and right.

Wiesel

refuseniks

Jackson

Falash

Abzug

Bader Ginsburg

Lieberman

Bernstein

ḥavurah

Priesand

Lilith

Sasso

Eilberg

```
W  R  E  T  N  E  T  E  D  U  H
C  X  R  Y  I  M  B  N  J  L  T
V  A  H  S  A  L  A  F  A  O  I
B  O  A  N  I  S  D  T  C  R  L
L  T  V  W  E  X  E  U  K  E  I
I  N  U  I  O  K  R  D  S  F  L
E  Y  R  P  O  M  G  E  O  U  T
B  P  A  E  R  W  I  J  N  S  R
E  C  H  P  O  W  N  T  R  E  M
R  T  Y  I  S  V  S  B  G  N  M
M  E  Q  E  S  C  B  O  L  I  H
A  S  W  R  A  B  U  P  I  K  J
N  I  E  T  S  N  R  E  B  S  C
E  I  L  B  E  R  G  U  Z  B  A
```

CHAPTER 9

CHALLENGES IN THE TWENTY-FIRST CENTURY

What, in your opinion, is the most critical issue facing American Jews in the twenty-first century? Why? How does this issue, and acting upon it, affect you?

T
he history of Jews in America has been one of ongoing challenges, arising from conditions both within and outside the community—and of changes designed to meet those new needs. There will never cease to be challenges, and the future of the American Jewish community depends upon how it faces them.

What the future holds, writes American Jewish historian Jonathan Sarna, no one knows. "That," he said, "will be determined day by day, community by community, Jew by Jew." But knowledge of the past, along with knowledge of Jewish law, tradition, custom, and values, can inform our choices and lead to effective and thoughtful action. The future of American Judaism depends on Jewish youth, the potential leaders of the community.

THE CHALLENGE OF INTERMARRIAGE

The Jewish birth rate, the number of Jews immigrating to the United States, and the number of people converting to Judaism are all dropping. The rate of intermarriage is up and children of intermarriages often identify either with Christianity or with no religion at all. This raises important questions for the Jewish community, including:

- What should the Jewish community's response be to these trends? Should the community attempt to affect these trends in some way? How might the community do that?

- Should the Jewish community consider intermarriage, as some people do, as an opportunity for outreach—a way to increase the number

of Jews—or should the community view it as a problem—given that the children of intermarriage sometimes do not identify as Jews?

- Jews have traditionally felt connected to and responsible for other Jews, wherever they may live. This feeling of *klal Yisra'el* has declined. What should the Jewish community do about this?

Think About It

What makes you feel part of *klal Yisra'el*?

THE CHALLENGE OF BOUNDARIES

The question of who is, or is not, considered part of the Jewish community—and the fact that the definition is different among the four movements of Judaism—is called a "boundary" issue. The rituals and obligations expected of converts differ, and who has the authority to accept someone as Jewish differs, with the Reconstructionist and Reform movements being more religiously liberal than the Orthodox and Conservative movements.

There are other boundary issues for the movements themselves. Can a woman who challenges traditional gender roles or

Choose one challenge that faced the Jewish community during its history in the United States. How was it handled? What lesson does it offer for the future?

Do It

someone who openly opposes Jewish tradition in some way be considered Orthodox? Can a synagogue or individual that does not accept the core beliefs and rituals of a particular movement be considered part of that movement? This situation leads to several challenges for the community:

- Is it possible for the movements to resolve such differences among themselves? How can Jews of different movements live together and create a strong, healthy, and vibrant community unless they resolve these issues?
- Where should compromises be made for the sake of unity and where should firm stands be made for the sake of principle?

 Think About It Do you believe there is one idea, or set of ideas, that defines the movement to which you belong and which must be accepted for a person to be considered part of that movement?

THE CHALLENGE OF AUTHORITY

Another challenge for the future of the Jewish community in America is the lack of an ultimate authority in Jewish life. No one rabbi, court, or group of lay leaders has the authority to make decisions for the entire community. Questions arise on a wide variety of issues, from whether to ordain gay and lesbian rabbis to the language of the liturgy. In addition, increasing numbers of Jews are making religious decisions on their own, without seeking the advice of any authority.

There are several questions concerning authority that the community must face:
- Should Jews strengthen religious authority or would it be better to promote autonomy among the major movements of Judaism in the United States?
- Is there a way to balance religious authority with personal **autonomy**?

 Learn It **Autonomy** means "independence."

 Think About It Are there questions that you would ask a chief rabbi if the American Jewish community had such a person?

THE CHALLENGE OF AMERICAN CULTURE

Some people feel that liberal American culture is at odds with traditional Jewish culture on such issues as sexual freedom, gender equality, gay and lesbian rights, and personal autonomy. Other American Jews insist that there is no incompatibility, and many have merged American and Jewish teachings. This dilemma arises for some American Jews at Ḥanukkah and Christmas, or when deciding whether to take off from school or miss a sporting event on a Jewish holiday or Shabbat. The challenge is how to balance American culture with Judaism, and what to do when they clash.

- In light of this challenge, when is it appropriate to compromise and when is it preferable and necessary to stand firm?
- What are the factors that go into making such a decision?

 Think About It What do you do when Judaism and American life clash? What has influenced you in making the decisions you have made? Are you completely satisfied with your decisions or do you wish you had acted differently? What help from others would you need to act differently in the future?

THE CHALLENGE OF ISRAEL

Israel has been important to American Jews since before the actual founding of the State in 1948. Given the political realities, there are questions that American Jews must ask themselves about Israel.
- How should American Jews officially relate to Israel?
- How will I relate to Israel?

A well-known ad campaign for bread echoes the cultural gap between Jews and non-Jews.

You don't have to be Jewish to love Levy's real Jewish Rye

Think About It

What actions could you take to support Israel?

THE CHALLENGE OF JEWISH CULTURE

There are many positive trends in the American Jewish community today. Jewish culture—literature, theater, art, dance, music, film, and television—all continue to grow in both quantity and quality. Jewish educational opportunities, from early childhood through adult lifelong learning, also continue to expand and improve. Synagogue life, in terms of both number of members and attendance, has blossomed. Synagogues are also trying to heighten spirituality and focus on formerly neglected groups. These positive developments raise questions for the community. For example:

- How should the community react to books, plays, television shows, or movies—either by Jews themselves or by non-Jews—that do not depict the Jewish community positively?
- How can the Jewish community encourage the growth and development of Jewish culture?
- What can Jewish communal leaders do to improve Jewish supplementary schools? Jewish day schools?

- What can synagogues do to heighten spirituality?
- What can synagogues do to pay greater attention to formerly neglected groups, such as gays and lesbians or single adults?

LOOKING INTO THE FUTURE

As Jewish life in the United States continues to be affected by events in America and worldwide, Jews will continue to find ways to meet the challenges that face them. How will you participate? How will you help your Jewish community, and the greater American Jewish community meet these challenges? How has your study of American Jewish history influenced you?

Do It

Conduct a Poll

Historian Jonathan Sarna points to several polls that have been conducted among American Jews to determine people's reactions to some of the issues described in this chapter. Conduct your own poll, asking people whether they agree, disagree, or have no opinion. Here are some of the statements you can include:

I look at the entire Jewish community as my extended family.

I have a special responsibility to take care of needy Jews around the world.

It is essential for Jews to marry other Jews.

I would be upset if my children were to convert to another religion.

It bothers me when people try to tell me that there is a right way to be Jewish.

It is important for Jews to be members of a synagogue.

Design additional statements of your own. Conduct the poll and share the results of your poll with the class. Ask the class: What have you learned?

UNIT 3 TIME LINE OF HISTORICAL EVENTS:
BEING JEWISH IN AMERICA TODAY

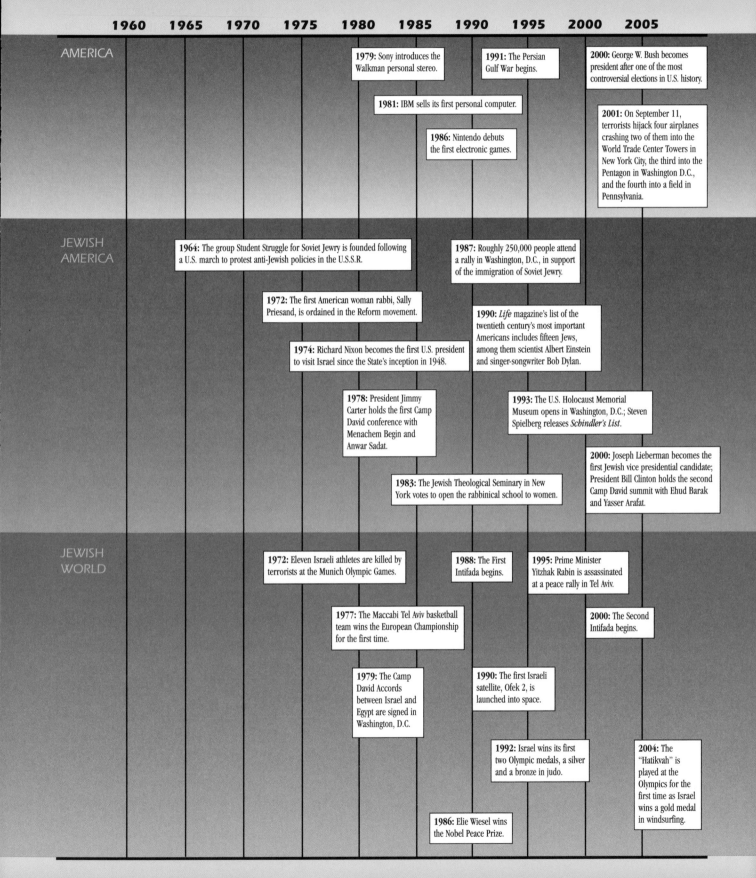

1960 **1965** **1970** **1975** **1980** **1985** **1990** **1995** **2000** **2005**

AMERICA

1979: Sony introduces the Walkman personal stereo.

1991: The Persian Gulf War begins.

2000: George W. Bush becomes president after one of the most controversial elections in U.S. history.

1981: IBM sells its first personal computer.

1986: Nintendo debuts the first electronic games.

2001: On September 11, terrorists hijack four airplanes crashing two of them into the World Trade Center Towers in New York City, the third into the Pentagon in Washington D.C., and the fourth into a field in Pennsylvania.

JEWISH AMERICA

1964: The group Student Struggle for Soviet Jewry is founded following a U.S. march to protest anti-Jewish policies in the U.S.S.R.

1987: Roughly 250,000 people attend a rally in Washington, D.C., in support of the immigration of Soviet Jewry.

1972: The first American woman rabbi, Sally Priesand, is ordained in the Reform movement.

1990: *Life* magazine's list of the twentieth century's most important Americans includes fifteen Jews, among them scientist Albert Einstein and singer-songwriter Bob Dylan.

1974: Richard Nixon becomes the first U.S. president to visit Israel since the State's inception in 1948.

1978: President Jimmy Carter holds the first Camp David conference with Menachem Begin and Anwar Sadat.

1993: The U.S. Holocaust Memorial Museum opens in Washington, D.C.; Steven Spielberg releases *Schindler's List*.

2000: Joseph Lieberman becomes the first Jewish vice presidential candidate; President Bill Clinton holds the second Camp David summit with Ehud Barak and Yasser Arafat.

1983: The Jewish Theological Seminary in New York votes to open the rabbinical school to women.

JEWISH WORLD

1972: Eleven Israeli athletes are killed by terrorists at the Munich Olympic Games.

1988: The First Intifada begins.

1995: Prime Minister Yitzhak Rabin is assassinated at a peace rally in Tel Aviv.

1977: The Maccabi Tel Aviv basketball team wins the European Championship for the first time.

2000: The Second Intifada begins.

1979: The Camp David Accords between Israel and Egypt are signed in Washington, D.C.

1990: The first Israeli satellite, Ofek 2, is launched into space.

1992: Israel wins its first two Olympic medals, a silver and a bronze in judo.

2004: The "Hatikvah" is played at the Olympics for the first time as Israel wins a gold medal in windsurfing.

1986: Elie Wiesel wins the Nobel Peace Prize.

Michael Alexander, Ph.D.

Michael Alexander is the Murray Friedman Professor of American Jewish History and the Director of the Feinstein Center for American Jewish History at Temple University. He is the author of *Jazz Age Jews*.

Murray Friedman, Ph.D.

Dr. Friedman is Director Emeritus of the Feinstein Center for American Jewish History at Temple University and of the Philadelphia Chapter of the American Jewish Committee, where he worked for forty-three years. He was vice chairman of the U.S. Commission on Civil Rights from 1986–1989. Dr. Friedman received his Ph.D. from Georgetown University in American political and social history. He has written numerous articles and books on American Jewish history. In 2005 Temple University created a Murray Friedman chair in American Jewish History in his honor.

Reena Sigman Friedman, Ph.D.

Dr. Reena Sigman Friedman is Associate Professor of Modern Jewish Civilization at the Reconstructionist Rabbinical College. She is the author of *These Are Our Children: Jewish Orphanages in the United States, 1880–1925* (1994) and numerous articles and publications. Dr. Friedman is also a faculty member of the Florence Melton Adult Mini-School.

Alice L. George, Ph.D.

After twenty years as an editor at newspapers such as the *Detroit Free Press* and the *Philadelphia Daily News,* Alice L. George left journalism to earn a Ph.D. in history at Temple University, which she received in 2001. Her award-winning doctoral dissertation has been turned into a book, *Awaiting Armageddon: How Americans Faced the Cuban Missile Crisis* (2003).

Nancy Isserman, Ph.D.

Nancy Isserman is the Director of the Challenge and Change: American Jewish History Curriculum Project, and the Associate Director of the Feinstein Center for American Jewish History at Temple University, where she has been since 1992. She received her Ph.D. in Political Science in 2005 from the Graduate Center, City University of New York. Her dissertation was entitled, *"I Harbor No Hate": A Study of Intolerance and Tolerance in Holocaust Survivors.* She holds an M.S.W. from the George Warren Brown School of Social Work at Washington University.

Nancy M. Messinger

Nancy Messinger has been the Director of Educational Resources at the Auerbach Central Agency for Jewish Education since 1987. She is also the website coordinator for www.acaje.org. Ms. Messinger earned a B.H.L. from the Jewish Theological Seminary, a certificate of Jewish librarianship from Gratz College, a B.S. in history from Columbia University, and an M.S. in counseling from Villanova University.

Julia Prymak

Julia Prymak is the owner of Pryme Design, a graphic design and production services company that manages all aspects of clients' print and promotional needs. She earned her B.F.A. from Rochester Institute of Technology.

Rochelle Buller Rabeeya

Rochelle Rabeeya is the Director of Educational Services at the Auerbach Central Agency for Jewish Education. She holds an M.A. and an honorary doctorate in Jewish education from Hebrew Union College–Jewish Institute of Religion and has done post-graduate studies in educational psychology. At ACAJE, she focuses on training school committees, helping schools develop a systemic approach to Jewish education, developing curriculums and coordinating staff development.

Shelley Kapnek Rosenberg, Ed.D.

Dr. Shelley Kapnek Rosenberg is the author of *Raising a Mensch: How to Bring Up Ethical Children in Today's World,* (2003) and *Adoption and the Jewish Family: Contemporary Perspectives* (1998). Dr. Rosenberg earned her Ed.D. in psychoeducational processes from Temple University. Since 1994, she has worked for the Auerbach Central Agency for Jewish Education.

Jonathan D. Sarna, Ph.D.

Jonathan D. Sarna is the Joseph H. and Belle R. Braun Professor of American Jewish History at Brandeis University. Dr. Sarna has written, edited, or co-edited twenty books. Articles, reviews, and commentaries by Dr. Sarna appear regularly in scholarly and popular journals, as well as in Jewish newspapers across North America. He is the author of *American Judaism: A History* (2004).

Helene Z. Tigay

Helene Z. Tigay has been the Executive Director of the Auerbach Central Agency for Jewish Education since 1990. She has a B.S. in psychology from Columbia University, a B.R.E. in Hebrew literature from the University of Pennsylvania, and has been in the doctoral program in psychological services at the University of Pennsylvania's Graduate School of Education. She has written articles on a variety of topics and is a recipient of the United Synagogue of Conservative Judaism's Ateret Kavod Award.